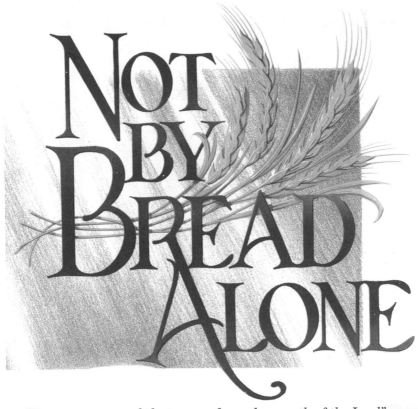

NOT BY BREAD ALONE

"But on every word that comes from the mouth of the Lord"
Deuteronomy 8:3

LCCN 93-78614
ISBN 1-56908-025-9

Art Work Copyright © 1993 C. Hawley
Co Editors - Sandy Farhart
Brenda Castro

Printed in the USA by

WIMMER
The Wimmer Companies, Inc.
Memphis • Dallas

Introduction

My appreciation to the hundreds of you from all over America that have made this book so dear to my heart. I invite you to use "Not By Bread Alone" in a way to bless your family and loved ones. Within its pages you will find the essence of hospitality to make your home a haven, a place of security where grace abounds. Graciousness is hospitality, kindness and love united. Kindness is a law unto itself and a result of a caring heart. Without love we are nothing, it is the only thing that will change a lonely world.

With the efforts of caring people, we can rekindle the hearts of those around us to light the world and make it a brighter inheritance for our children. This can be done by having a warm dinner prepared for our family each evening, to taking a pot of red beans to a sick neighbor. All that is needed is a willing spirit and a caring heart.

God's richest blessings on each of you.

Be not forgetful to entertain
the stranger:
for thereby some have
entertained angels
unaware.
Hebrews 13:2

John and Diana Hagee

John Hagee Ministries is a multi-faceted evangelistic ministry reaching millions with the good news of the gospel of Jesus Christ and calling America back to Bible-based Christianity.

Global Evangelism Television, Inc., the media outreach of John Hagee Ministries, produces three TV programs: *Cornerstone*, a weekly one-hour broadcast carried on Christian networks and major cable networks such as superstation WGN, as well as local stations; *John Hagee Today*, a thirty-minute program carried Monday-Friday on cable networks and local stations; and *Cornerstone Live*, a live satellite broadcast of the Sunday evening service at Pastor Hagee's church in San Antonio, Texas.

John Hagee Ministries TV programs are seen coast to coast and from Canada to the Caribbean. Cable television broadcasts reach into 90 million homes across America. The live Sunday night broadcast can be picked up by over five million homes with backyard satellite dishes.

Cornerstone Church was founded in 1975 with just 25 members. Within two years a new sanctuary was built seating 1,600. The spirit of evangelism brought new converts into the Kingdom and explosive growth to the church body. In 1987 a new 5,000 seat church was built for the nondenominational congregation. Multiple services are held each Sunday for the 10,000+ members of Cornerstone.

John Hagee is one of America's leading pastors, as well as a scholar, musician, athlete and evangelist. Author of several books, he is a popular conference speaker whose straightforward style of preaching, laced with humor, brings refreshing biblical insight to contemporary problems.

When he surrendered to the call of God at age seventeen, John Hagee laid aside his life's desire to be an attorney and became a fourth-generation preacher in the tradition of his father and grandfathers. He is also pastor to other pastors around the country through the Cornerstone Fellowship of Churches.

The burning passion of Pastor Hagee's heart is world evangelism and he believes that television is one of the most powerful means of spreading the gospel ever known. He also preaches major crusades at home and in foreign countries.

In addition to running the incredibly busy Hagee household, Diana Castro Hagee oversees the daily operation of the television ministry. She travels extensively with her husband and speaks to pastor's wives and lay leaders at ministry events.

Gifted with a gracious spirit of hospitality, Diana Hagee frequently opens her home and her heart to ministry staff and visitors. On these occasions her kitchen becomes a bustling beehive of activity issuing forth mouth-watering morsels of nourishing food served in the love and fellowship of Jesus Christ.

John and Diana Hagee live in San Antonio, Texas with their children Tish, Chris, Christina, Matthew and Sandy.

Cookbook Committee

Diana Hagee, C.O.S. Global Evangelism Publishing

Sandy Farhart, Co-chairman, Editor

Brenda Castro, Co-chairman, Editor

Jo Wagner

Dorothy Schuhmacher

Dee Dee Kloppe

Cora Spitz

Billie Tsukifuji

Table of Contents

Dedication

This book is dedicated to the special people in my life. The Corner-stone Church family whose love and acceptance have made my life a thing of joy. To my mother, Velia Castro, who taught me how to cook and to love to care for my family. To my sister, Sandy Farhart, and my sister-in-law, Brenda Castro, who worked endless hours on this project. To our wonderful children who have always made me feel like a gourmet cook. To my husband, whose love and encouragement have given me confidence. To my Lord who has shown me what unconditional love is—His Word is truly the "bread of life".

SERVING...
SHOWING CHRIST'S LOVE

If anyone gives even a cup of cold water
to one of these little ones because he is my disciple,
I tell you the truth, he will certainly not lose his reward.
MATTHEW 10. 42

MINISTRY OF HELPS

The Ministry of Helps

"He humbled you, causing you to hunger and then feeding you with manna, which neither you nor your fathers had known, to teach you that man does not live on bread alone but on every word that comes from the mouth of the Lord." (Deut. 8:3 NIV)

Man's life consists of more than what he eats. He is nurtured and sustained by the love of his family, the joy of his children, the laughter of a baby, the peace that comes from God and the kindness of friends and neighbors.

These elements were readily found in the American home in times past. As a child, you were thrilled when your family would "have company over." Your mother would prepare all day for the special visitors who were coming to your home. Dad would make sure to be home from work on time so he could welcome them at the door. You would help Mom set the table with the family's best, not to show off your possessions but to make sure that your guests were treated to your very best while in your home.

If you were lucky, you would be allowed to stay in the living room as these special friends laughed and told stories with your parents. As the evening came to a close, you would feel a little sad to see your company leave. But you knew that soon another set of friends would be welcomed through the portals of your home to be honored guests at your table.

Each of us has wonderful memories of sitting on the front porch of Grandma's house on a warm summer night, eating watermelon, drinking ice tea or sipping lemonade. The evening was remembered not so much for the menu but for the laughter, the security, the joy and the happiness.

Do you remember the picnics on the Fourth of July when you would invite all the neighbors and they would come with great offerings of their favorite dishes? Joy and laughter would make the day a memory that would last forever.

Can you remember the days your mother would prepare a pot of soup for a friend who was ill? The sick friend may not have felt like eating, but the joy of receiving such a labor of love soon put him or her on the road to recovery.

Yes, those were the days, when we lived by every word that comes from the mouth of the Lord and tasted the fruit that came from the trees of love, joy, kindness and hospitality. As long as those memories live in our minds and hearts, then there is the possibility of reviving an America known for its open doors and gracious hospitality.

As a pastor's wife, I have seen the wounds of grief soothed by the balm of kindness when a chicken casserole arrived at the home of a family that had just experienced the passing of a loved one. Little things mean a lot!

We can replace the acts of hostility and anger we witness daily on the evening news with acts of kindness and love. Food plays a very important role in a revival of fractured relationships.

As For Me and My House

Hospitality begins at home. The rule at our home is that we eat the evening meal together. That may sound a bit too fundamental but in the mobile society in which we live, it's a great accomplishment just to have your family together around the dinner table.

During our meal, we discuss the events of the day, trying to concentrate on the children as much as possible. We struggle to keep the laughter which dominates any topic brought to the table to a low roar. Usually the more serious Mom tries to be, the more the children consider it a challenge to make laughter the goal.

I know they will remember the dinner long after they forget what I served, because the joy and security that comes from that special time together will never be forgotten. I always feel honored when they ask, as they often do, if they may invite a friend over to dinner.

Much to my dismay, I've found that having dinner at home around the table in America has become an endangered species.

I know that many of you are working mothers and are often overwhelmed by your busy schedules. I know how it is—I've been there. I've been blessed by having a very understanding husband and terrific kids who are very willing to adjust to hectic schedules.

My first rule is this: don't allow yourself to feel overwhelmed! The meal will get done if you plan properly. When you have a light day, plan to make several main dishes for future meals. These can be anything from casseroles to spaghetti sauce to chili and taco meat.

Store these in your freezer and plan the week's menu around them. You'll find that selecting a previously prepared main dish from your freezer in the morning, then adding a salad, bread and a vegetable to the meal that night will make your evenings at home a lot less stressful.

Another helpful hint is to set the table before you leave for work in the morning. Doing this task in advance will allow you to put your feet up for awhile before you serve dinner. The less stress you experience, the more the dinner hour will be a pleasant experience for you and your family.

You might say to me, "Diana, I hate to cook!" But you don't have to enjoy cooking to put together a really great meal for yourself or your family. Always remember that you are doing more than sustaining life with food: you are creating an atmosphere of love and security in an otherwise stressful environment.

You will find some really terrific and easy recipes in this cookbook to help make your life easy and the contribution you make to your family one of excellence.

Mi Casa Es Su Casa

With my Mexican heritage, it is second nature for me to equate hospitality with food. "My home is your home" was our family motto as we opened our home to guests. Little did I know that this gift of hospitality would influence not only my future home, but also the church I would eventually help pastor with my husband.

When I first married, I went through a time of feeling absolutely inadequate as a pastor's wife. I had little training in the art of being a pastor's wife. I couldn't sing in tune, couldn't play the piano or the organ and didn't have a life changing teaching ministry. What could I do?

With the help of my husband, a loving congregation and our gracious Lord, I was able to realize that I had been given the gift of hospitality. I loved to entertain and to make people feel at home, giving them a part of myself by opening the doors of our home.

When we began our church, the congregation only numbered 25. Our active membership now exceeds 13,000. Some may think that the growth was spontaneous, but it was not. Through the anointed preaching of the word of God, a tremendous pastoral staff and the grace of God, our church has been blessed with continuous growth. When our church was still very small, we decided to have people come to our home after every Sunday evening service. We were on an extremely tight budget, so our menus were very simple—yet they were crowd pleasers.

Our objective was to invite families we had not previously met. Our guests did not care what they were served...they were not concerned with the condition of my home...they were just thrilled to be together with the pastor's family. I remember how my husband and I would pray before they arrived, "Lord, bless our guests as they walk through the door of our home. Let them feel your presence, your comfort and your joy. If they need healing, then heal them through us. If they need companionship, then let us fill the loneliness in their lives. We ask that your love be felt in this home. Allow each guest to be fed—body, soul and spirit."

The Lord never failed. We always had enough to "feed the multitudes" and there was always more than enough food and love to go around.

Please don't think that you have to be a pastor's wife to open your home to people you don't know very well or even to those with whom you would like to develop a better relationship. Whatever your station in life, your hospitality is always appreciated. With a little desire and organization, you can become a successful hostess.

Here are some very simple steps to begin your adventure into hospitality.

1. Decide who you would like to invite to dinner. Consider family friends, or someone from your workplace or maybe a neighbor.

2. Invite your guests at a time that will be easy on your schedule. Don't create additional stress!

3. Plan your menu several days in advance. The more elaborate your menu, the farther ahead you need to plan. Planning menus is very enjoyable for me. I lie in bed at night after the children are asleep and look through cookbooks for recipe ideas.

Make sure to plan a menu that is within your budget. Choose something that is not difficult to prepare and try not to get too exotic. "Home cooking" in itself is becoming a rarity.

4. Make your grocery list. Be careful not to buy duplicates of what you already have on your shelf. Be sure to check the spices you have on hand. They are rather expensive and you usually end up with four cans of oregano because you didn't take the time to look in the pantry before you made your grocery list.

5. Do your shopping two to three days before your dinner. Don't wait to do this too close to your date—then you will overwork yourself with lots of running around. Take your time and enjoy shopping.

6. Please remember that if you are on a tight budget, you don't have to worry. With the right attitude and a spark of creativity, you can make a little go a long way. I consider it a challenge to make a really great meal at minimal cost because I always want to be a good steward of our money.

7. If there is any part of your menu you can make ahead of time, do so the day before your dinner. Unless I am preparing for a large group, I usually don't make something too far ahead of time because of storage problems...and the over-anxious nibblers who sneak bites before the party.

8. Set the table the night before. This is almost a must. You would be surprised how much time you save by doing this early, not to mention the peace of mind that comes from knowing this time-consuming task is done.

9. Plan a time schedule for the dishes you are going to prepare. This will help you get your meal ready on time. Let me give you a secret. I've found that my phone has a horrible little habit of ringing all day when I am trying to prepare diner. I simple call the V.I.P. in my life, tell them all is well, and let them know that I will be disconnecting my phone for the next few hours until my mission is accomplished. Then I put on some soothing, inspirational music and have a great time preparing for my guests.

10. Try and have your meal ready one hour before your company arrives. This leaves thirty minutes to get ready and thirty minutes to relax before your guests arrive.

11. Almost without fail, your guests will ask if they can help. I always say, "Not now, but you can help with the dishes later." I usually find that the best visiting time with them is during our clean-up chores. We begin to let our hair down and friendships begin to develop as your guests feel they are really a part of your home during this personal time in your kitchen. It's also especially helpful if you have to go to work the next morning.

Always feel good about opening your home to your guests. They will not want to leave.

As you begin to open your home to others, keep in mind that many people have become hardened in order to protect themselves from rejection. They draw circles around themselves to keep people out. But with God's help, you can draw these people into your circle of love and give them the gift of acceptance.

I admire our Jewish friends for the beautiful Sabbath tradition of having a guest in their home during this sacred time together. This is a prime example of expanding your circle of love. My husband and I have shared "bringing in the Sabbath" in many Jewish homes and it has always been a blessing. Not only because of the wonderful dishes that were prepared with such love and care, but also because of the warm feeling of acceptance we have felt in their homes.

Cast Your Bread Upon the Water

I can't begin to tell you the importance of taking the kindness that you have in your home and sharing it with the people who live around you. There are several different ways to do this.

First, you must make up your mind that you want to reach outside your home. With this purpose in mind, you will make your neighbors feel comfortable as they accept your sincere effort of friendship. If someone new moves into your neighborhood, take over your favorite dessert and draw them into your circle of hospitality. Moving into a new area can be very stressful, and you can help them feel very welcome in their new home.

Any time you know someone in your neighborhood is ill, call and let them know you want to prepare a meal for them. Ask when you may bring it over. You will be overwhelmed at the pleasant response you'll receive.

Our church members participate in a program called "home ministries". Groups of four or five families gather in homes one evening each week for Bible study and fellowship. This program serves two main purposes.

First, it allows a large congregation to develop close friendships in a more intimate setting. Every member of the home ministry brings a covered dish assigned to her or him by the head of the ministry. As people break bread together they begin to trust and love one another.

Secondly, this program helps the church to meet the needs of families. I've seen families transformed by the kindness they've felt when members of their home ministry brought food during an illness or reached out to them in other practical ways.

One of the most touching scenes however, has been at the homes of those who have had a death in the family. Even though we believe that death is a coronation in the world to come, we know that grieving is very natural at the passing of a loved one.

When we learn there is a death in the family, someone from the church arrives in the home within the hour. Food continues to be brought every day, ending the day of the funeral service. Not only do we bring food but we also bring the labor that goes with serving, cleaning and greeting those visiting the home to pay their respects to the family. Grief is natural and must be experienced before true healing can begin. Bringing food to the home is truly medicine for the heart at such a trying time.

If your church does not have a similar program, perhaps you should think of starting one. If you do not attend church, then the next time you hear of a friend or neighbor who has had a death in the family, bless their home with food. It will make a dark day brighter!

Another place you can minister through food is at the hospital. A dear friend of ours had major surgery in a city about 90 miles away. A friend of mine suggested we take a basket of snacks and beverages to make the long waiting period for the family easier.

Always ready for a new adventure, we did just that. It worked miracles. The family did not want to leave the waiting room for fear the doctors would return with news of their loved one, so the basket of food not only provided the necessary sustenance but also served as a distraction from a very stressful experience.

Allow me to suggest one more avenue of ministry through food. When a relative, friend or neighbor is in financial difficulty, don't forget food. If you have your pantry stocked, then you can spend that bit of extra money on their bills that must be paid. Simply go to your own pantry and prepare a basket of food or fill the basket with food staples you purchase at the grocery store. Not only does it serve a practical purpose, it also provides a tremendous amount of moral support to someone going through trying times.

There are many different methods you can use to minister through food. The important thing is to just be willing to try. You'll be pleasantly surprised how creative you can become when you have purposed to be a vessel of kindness.

Feeding the Multitudes

Needless to say, there are many gatherings of the multitudes that occur in our church and in our home every year. My husband and I calculated that over the last seven years, we have entertained well over 10,000 people in our home. From wedding rehearsal dinners and bridal showers to festive banquets, we've had them all and truly enjoyed them. Our goal is to always make people feel welcomed when they arrive and satisfied when they leave.

Am I suggesting you must entertain thousands of people before you can feel that you have opened your home? Absolutely not! But don't be afraid of large gatherings. You may never feel comfortable in having large crowds in your home, and that's fine…it's definitely not for everyone. But for those of you who have been toying with the idea, allow me to give you some helpful hints that will make large gatherings easier for you.

1. Determine the purpose of your event. This will help you plan your budget, menu and decorations.

2. How many people do you want to have? Don't overdo it the first time out. Choose a number you're comfortable with and which can easily be accommodated within your budget.

3. What is your budget? This is essential in choosing your menu. Depending on the number of people and the kind of event you're having, your budget should be easily attainable. You would be surprised how many different crowd-pleasing menus you can plan that will be easy on your budget. In addition to your menu, there are several other things to consider when preparing your budget.

• Will your event be indoors or outdoors? This will determine where your guests will sit and whether you will need additional chairs.

• Is it a casual event or a formal one? This will let you know if you should use paper goods or rent dinnerware.

- Are you mailing invitations or calling your guests? If you send invitations, will they be store bought or custom printed? Don't forget to include your mailing costs.

- Plan the menu. By answering the questions above, you will have the basic format of your menu. I try to plan the menu several days ahead of my event so that I can be totally tension-free in choosing the foods to be served. Plan on making dishes with which you're familiar. A dinner party is not the time to try out new menus.

4. One of the main things to consider when planning a menu is how to begin your evening. I like to have a refreshing drink when guests arrived. This not only allows them to relax, it also gives you time to put the finishing touches on your menu. Follow the beverages with appetizers if you wish. Appetizers are great for longer evenings, but if you are entertaining on a weeknight, you probably want to serve your meal shortly after your guests arrive.

Here is an example of a typical menu for a large party in my home:

1. Appetizer and drink
2. Two main dishes
3. Two salads
4. Three vegetables
5. Two desserts
6. Bread and butter
7. Tea and coffee

This general menu is recommended for groups of 20 or more. When the number of guests exceeds 50, I use different menus. These can include an all appetizer menu or a theme menu such as taco bars or hot dog and hamburger stations. Again, be creative and practical in planning your menus.

5. Make your grocery list. If you are making a meal for a large crowd this could mean more than one trip to the store, so plan accordingly.

6. If you need to make phone calls to rental agencies or print shops, meat markets or specialty shops, allow plenty of time in your schedule for these arrangements. Think realistically and remember to allow extra time for unexpected delays.

7. A preparation timetable is essential to any size meal, but critical to a large gathering. In preparing your timetable, consider the following

questions.

- Where will I store the groceries I buy ahead of time?

- Do I have enough refrigerator or freezer space? If not, can a friend or neighbor help me with storage?

- How many people will help me prepare and serve this meal, if any? When will they arrive and what responsibilities do they have? How will this affect my timetable?

- What time will my deliveries be made? Have I written checks or prepared envelopes with cash in them ahead of time so there will be no confusion the day of the delivery?

- What time do I decorate the serving tables with cloths and serving dishes?

- How long does each item on my menu take to prepare? In what order should they be prepared and when should each dish be ready?

- What time do I begin to serve?

- In what containers will I store leftovers? Plastic freezer bags are handy for this project. They are relatively inexpensive and they can easily fit into your refrigerator or freezer.

- Also prepare a clean-up plan. This should include the time that any delivery service will come to pick up rented items. And don't forget to plan for handling garbage. This is a common problem after a large meal, especially if you use paper products. Buy several extra garbage bags with strong ties if your garbage pick-up is not the day after your event.

This may seem like a lot of trouble. However, filling out this schedule can make an otherwise difficult task a pleasure.

Whether preparing for two or 200, it is important not to lose sight of your purpose. When you remain focused on your goal, everything else will fall into place. Each time you have people in your home, your main goal should be to provide an atmosphere of gracious hospitality. Then your home will become known as an outpost in a society looking for a revival of family values and true brotherhood.

The following suggested menus cover all types of meal planning or ministry examples I have shared with you. Keep in mind when reading these menus that I have tried them all and recommend them highly... however, there is nothing better than an original idea by the cook herself!

Favorite "Company's Coming" Menu

Serves 8

Piña Colada Appetizer Drinks (page 75)

Cream of Crab Soup

Green Goddess Salad

Cornish Game Hens with Wild Rice Dressing

Whole Green Beans

Glazed Carrots

Pineapple Pound Cake

Tea and Coffee

Rolls

Cream of Crab Soup

2 10¾-ounce cans cream of mushroom soup, undiluted
2 10¾-ounce cans cream of asparagus soup, undiluted
3 soup cans milk
2 cups half and half
2 6½-ounce cans flaked crab meat or 1 pound fresh crab meat
½ cup sherry
½ cup diced pimiento

Combine mushroom and asparagus soups, milk and half and half in large saucepan. Bring to a low boil. Add crab and beat well. Stir in sherry and pimiento. Heat for 1 minute. Serve hot.

Green Goddess Salada

Combine lettuce, artichokes, olives, cucumber and tomatoes. Drizzle Green Goddess dressing over vegetables or serve salad on individual serving plates and offer dressing.

10 cups torn leaf lettuce, chilled
2 7-ounce jars marinated artichokes, drained
1 cup pitted black olives
1 cup sliced cucumber
3 medium-sized tomatoes, cut in wedges

Green Goddess Dressing

Combine mayonnaise, onion and parsley. Combine tarragon vinegar, crushed tarragon and anchovies in blender container. Process briefly and add to mayonnaise mixture. Chill for about 4 hours.

2 cups mayonnaise
⅔ cup minced green onion with tops
3 tablespoons minced parsley
3 tablespoons tarragon vinegar
1 tablespoon crushed tarragon
2 anchovy filets

Cornish Game Hens

8 Cornish game hens
2 teaspoons margarine
2 tablespoons minced garlic
Seasoned salt to taste
Coarsely ground black pepper to taste

Wash and rinse hens, blotting with paper towel to dry. Combine margarine and garlic. Rub on hens and season generously with seasoned salt and black pepper. Place in roasting pan. Bake at 350° for 1 hour or until golden brown and leg joint moves easily.

Wild Rice Dressing

1¼ cups wild rice
Chicken broth
1 12-ounce package bulk pork sausage
1 4-ounce can sliced mushrooms
1 teaspoon salt
¼ teaspoon black pepper
1 10¾-ounce can cream of mushroom soup, undiluted
1 medium-sized onion, diced
1 tablespoon minced garlic
1 4-ounce jar pimiento
1 tablespoon sugar
1 teaspoon seasoned salt
⅓ cup slivered almonds

Prepare rice according to package directions, using chicken broth as liquid. Sauté sausage, stirring to crumble, until brown. Drain excess fat. Combine sausage, wild rice, mushrooms, salt and black pepper. Combine soup, onion, garlic, pimiento, sugar, seasoned salt and almonds. Add rice mixture and mix well. Spread mixture in buttered 2½-quart casserole. Bake at 350° for 45 minutes.

Glazed Carrots

**2 pounds small
  carrots
  Salted water
2 tablespoons
  margarine
1 tablespoon vanilla
½ cup firmly-packed
  brown sugar
¼ teaspoon nutmeg**

*Cook carrots in salted water until
tender. Drain well. Combine margarine, vanilla, brown sugar and nutmeg
in saucepan. Cook, stirring often, until
bubbly. Place carrots in 12x8x2-inch
baking dish. Pour sugar mixture over
carrots, turning to coat thoroughly.
Bake at 350° for 30 minutes.*

Pineapple Pound Cake

**Cake
  2¾ cups sugar
  ½ cup vegetable
    shortening
  1 cup butter or
    margarine, softened
  6 eggs
  3 cups all-purpose
    flour
  1 teaspoon baking
    powder
  ¼ cup milk
  1 teaspoon vanilla
  ¾ cup drained
    crushed pineapple**

*Cream sugar, shortening and butter
together until light and fluffy. Add
eggs, 1 at a time, beating well after
each addition. Combine flour and
baking powder. Alternately add dry
ingredients and milk and vanilla,
beating well after each addition. Stir
in pineapple. Pour batter into well
greased and floured 10-inch tube pan.
Bake at 325° for 1 hour and 15 minutes or until wooden pick inserted near
center comes out clean. Cool in pan for
15 minutes and invert on serving plate.
Drizzle glaze over top and sides of
cake.*

**Glaze
  ¼ cup melted
    margarine or butter
  1½ cups powdered
    sugar
  1 cup drained
    crushed pineapple**

*Combine butter and sugar, mixing
until smooth. Stir in pineapple. Drizzle
glaze over cake.*

Note: *Do not preheat oven. Pineapple
juice may be substituted for milk.*

Rolls

2 **envelopes dry active yeast**
3 **cups warm (110° to 115°) water, divided**
¾ **cup sugar**
1 **cup all bran cereal**
1 **cup margarine or butter**
6 **cups all-purpose flour, divided**
2 **eggs**
1½ **teaspoons salt**
¼ **cup milk**
   Melted butter

Dissolve yeast in 2 cups warm water. Add sugar and cereal. Using pastry blender or forks, cut margarine into 3 cups flour. Add yeast mixture and 1 cup warm water. Beat eggs with salt and add with milk to batter. Stir in about 3 cups flour to form soft dough. Let rise, covered, until doubled in bulk. Punch down and chill until ready to prepare rolls. On lightly floured surface, roll dough, a small amount at a time, to ¼-inch thickness. Cut with biscuit cutter or glass, brush with melted butter, fold and place on baking sheet. Let rise until doubled in bulk. Bake at 325° until golden brown.

Hospital Basket

Any large straw basket
Roll of summer sausage
Small brick of smoked Cheddar cheese
Crackers
Fruit juices
Mineral water
Assorted fruit
Pound cake
Pretzels
Candy
Small paper plates
Small paper cups
Small paring knife
Napkins

Arrange in basket and take to the family members waiting while their loved ones are in surgery.

Summer Patio Party

For 25 to 30 Guests

Shrimp Pasta

Spinach Quiche

Crab Quiche

Honey Baked Ham

Smoked Turkey Breast

Banana Bread (page 99)

Fruit Salad (page 69)

Chocolate Caramel Brownies (page 200)

Tea

Shrimp Pasta

1 16-ounce package spaghetti
Water
Salt to taste
2 pounds fresh or frozen medium shrimp, cooked and peeled
2 tablespoons minced garlic
1 stalk celery, diced
1 7-ounce jar pimiento
1 16-ounce package frozen peas
4 cups mayonnaise
Seasoned salt to taste

Prepare spaghetti according to package directions, breaking pasta before cooking. Drain well. Add shrimp and garlic, tossing to mix thoroughly. Combine celery, pimiento, peas, mayonnaise and seasoned salt. Add to spaghetti mixture, mixing lightly but well. Chill until ready to serve. Yield: 8 servings.

Spinach Quiche

- 1 **unbaked 10-inch pastry shell**
- 1 **medium-sized onion, diced**
- 2 **teaspoons margarine**
- 2 **4-ounce cans sliced mushrooms, drained**
- 2 **cups (8 ounces) grated Monterey Jack cheese**
- 2 **10-ounce packages frozen spinach soufflé, thawed**

Place pastry in 10-inch pie pan. Sauté onion in margarine until transparent. Add mushrooms to onion and sauté for 2 minutes. Sprinkle cooked vegetables in pastry shell. Sprinkle cheese on vegetables. Place spinach on cheese, pressing lightly to completely cover cheese. Bake at 350° for 45 minutes or until knife tip inserted near center comes out clean. Yield: 6 to 8 servings.

Crab Quiche

- 4 **eggs, beaten**
- 1 **cup half and half**
- 1 **teaspoon seasoned salt**
- ¾ **teaspoon salt**
  Dash of cayenne pepper
- 2 **tablespoons mayonnaise**
- 1 **cup (4 ounces) grated Swiss cheese**
- 1 **cup (4 ounces) grated Cheddar cheese**
- 1 **tablespoon all-purpose flour**
- 2 **6½-ounce cans flaked crab meat**
- 1 **unbaked 10-inch pastry shell**
  Paprika

Combine eggs and half and half. Add seasoned salt, salt, cayenne pepper and mayonnaise. Combine Swiss and Cheddar cheeses, flour and crab. Add crab mixture to egg liquid, mixing well. Pour into pastry shell and sprinkle with paprika. Bake at 325° for 45 to 60 minutes or until knife tip inserted near center comes out clean. Yield: 6 to 8 servings

Iced Tea Base

Bring water to boil in large saucepan. Add tea bags, bring to a boil, then remove from heat and let steep for 15 minutes. Stir in sugar, bring to a boil and cook for 2 to 3 minutes. Cool to room temperature. Pour into jar and store in refrigerator. Cooled liquid will be consistency of syrup. To serve, place 1⅓ cups tea base in 1-gallon pitcher and fill with water. Serve over ice. Yield: 4 gallons

4 cups water
12 family size tea bags
4 cups sugar
Water

Mexican Fiesta

Serves 100

All of these recipes are found in the chapter on Mexican recipes. To attain the necessary servings, simply calculate how many times to repeat the recipe for the number of guests.

Appetizers

Hot Sauce

Chile con Queso

Ceviche

Tostadas

Piña Colada

Buffet

Chicken Fajitas

Beef Fajitas

Mexican Rice

Frijoles Borrachos

Flour Tortillas

Tea

Condiments

Pico de Gallo

Guacamole

Grated Cheese

Sour Cream

Dessert

Pastel de Queso (Full Cheesecake Bar)

Flow is essential to your gathering. Set at least four tables to present your "Mexican Fiesta". If you have the space, you can even be more effective. Nevertheless, where there is a will, there's a way. Have a great party.

The following chapter is from many generations of Mexican cooking. I sincerely hope you will enjoy making these treasured recipes for your family.

EVERY MEXICAN DISH I EVER MADE

and relished!

DIANA'S MEXICAN BUFFET

Mexican food is an ethnic food that transcends cultural boundaries, bringing people together in the spirit of fiesta. It is a great crowd pleaser.

Though it is very special, Mexican food is easily prepared. Most ingredients are found in your kitchen and are very inexpensive. Remember, Mexican food is very colorful, as well as flavorful, so be creative.

Historically, a Mexican home comes together around the evening meal. Because it is economical to prepare, you can always invite friends and neighbors in for a mini-fiesta.

As I begin to tour you through my kitchen, allow me to share with you some common ingredients found in all Mexican kitchens.

Frijoles or pinto beans. *The most popular Mexican bean in Texas, they come dried, cooked whole or refried, in your store. In your home, they are cooked slowly with a soupy broth, mashed or refried.*

Arroz or rice. *A long grain rice is best used to prepare the most popular side dish in Mexican food.*

Cebolla or onion. *It can be white, yellow or green and is used in most dishes.*

Tomate or tomatoes. *You need to have plenty of these red juicy vegetables on hand. They are used abundantly in Mexican foods. Remember, tomatoes can also be found in cans, either stewed or crushed.*

Queso or cheese. *Cheese is a must! I use a variety of long horn Cheddar, Monterey Jack or mozzarella. The new low-fat varieties work very well.*

Ajo or garlic. *Garlic is an essential spice for Mexican dishes. You may find fresh garlic in the produce section of your grocery store. I find it in a jar on the grocery shelf as well. You can ask for chopped or minced fresh garlic, a fantastic modern convenience.*

Comino or cumin or comino seed. *I prefer the powder. This too is a must seasoning for most dishes.*

Cilantro or coriander. *It comes in seed or fresh leaf form. Cilantro (also known as Chinese parsley) resembles parsley and is in the fresh produce section of your grocery. All uses in this chapter will be in the fresh form.*

Chilies or peppers. *What would we do without these wonderful spicy additions to our menus!*

- **Chili powder.** *A blend of dried ground chilies with added seasonings like cumin and oregano. Easily found on your grocery shelf.*

- **Anaheim chili pepper.** *Long, green and flavorful. These chilies are found fresh in the produce section or canned (whole or diced). They are usually mild but sometimes you will get a hot batch so be cautious. When I refer to "green chilies" or "canned chilies", I refer to Anaheim.*

- **Serrano chili pepper.** *Small, thin chilies. These are very hot! Can be found fresh or canned.*

- **Jalapeño chili pepper.** *Larger and fatter than serrano. Also found fresh or canned. Jalapeño peppers are usually found pickled when canned.*

My desire is for you to enjoy making and serving Mexican food as well as eating it. As you read through the next few pages, begin to plan a special meal for your family or friends and enjoy, as in Spanish, Buen Provecho.

Antojitos

Appetizers

1. *Antojito de Aceituna — Olive Relish Dip*
2. *Antojito de Frijoles — Bean Dip*
3. *Ceviche — Fish Appetizer*
4. *Antojito de Camaron — Shrimp Appetizer*
5. *Camaron a la Vinagreta — Shrimp with Vinegar*
6. *Chile Con Queso — Cheese with Peppers*
7. *Flautas — Flutes (Crispy Rolled Tacos)*
8. *Guacamole — Avocado Dip or Salad*
9. *Jalea de Jalapeño — Jalapeño Jelly*
10. *Jalapeños Rellenos — Stuffed Jalapeños*
11. *Pico de Gallo — Roosters Beak (Fresh Chunky Salsa)*
12. *Nachos — Tortilla Chips with Melted Cheese*
13. *Quesadillas — Cheese Filled Tortillas*
14. *Queso Flameado — Cheese with Sausage*
15. *Queso Fundido — Cheese with onion, Mushrooms and Chilies*
16. *Salsa Verde*
17. *Salsas — Hot Sauce*
18. *Taquitos — Little Tacos*
19. *Tostadas — Fried Tortilla Chips*

Antojito de Aceituna

Olive Relish Dip

6 green onions, diced
2 large firm tomatoes, diced
2 4-ounce cans ripe olives, chopped
2 4-ounce cans green chilies, chopped
1 cup Italian salad dressing or vinegar and oil dressing
Tostados

Combine onion, tomatoes, olives and chilies. Pour dressing over vegetables and chill for 2 hours before serving. Serve with Tostados (page 43). Yield: 6 to 8 servings.

Variation: *To reduce fat grams, use non-fat Italian salad dressing.*

Antojito de Frijoles

Bean Dip

Heat refried beans in saucepan. Stir in tomatoes with chilies, garlic and cumin and heat thoroughly. Stir in cheese and simmer until cheese is melted. Add sour cream. Serve warm with Tostados (page 43). Yield: 8 to 10 servings.

Variation: To reduce fat grams in dish, use non-fat refried beans, low-fat cheese and low-fat sour cream. Serve with Non-Fat Tostados (page 43).

- **2 cups refried beans**
- **1 10-ounce can tomatoes with chilies, diced**
- **½ teaspoon minced garlic**
- **½ teaspoon cumin**
- **1 cup (4 ounces) grated Cheddar cheese**
- **½ cup sour cream Tostados**

Ceviche

Fish Appetizer

Poach fish in lightly salted water until fish flakes easily. Drain, let stand until cool and cut into bite-sized pieces. Combine fish, lemon juice, olives, green chilies, onion, tomatoes, cilantro, oregano and oil, tossing to coat fish evenly with dressing. Chill for about 2 hours. Serve cold with Tostados (page 43). Yield: 10 to 12 servings.

Variation: Shrimp and scallops may be substituted for fish for a seafood ceviche.

- **1½ pounds orange roughy or mild, firm fish Salted water**
- **1 cup fresh lemon or lime juice**
- **1 cup pimiento-stuffed green olives, chopped**
- **2 4-ounce cans green chilies, seeded and chopped**
- **½ cup chopped green onion**
- **2 large ripe tomatoes, diced**
- **½ cup fresh chopped cilantro**
- **¼ teaspoon oregano**
- **¼ cup olive oil Tostados**

Antojito de Camaron

Shrimp Appetizer

2½ quarts boiling
    water
¼ cup lime juice,
    divided
1 bay leaf
2 tablespoons minced
    garlic
1 teaspoon salt
⅛ teaspoon cayenne
    pepper
2 pounds fresh
    shrimp
1 4-ounce can green
    chilies, chopped
1 large tomato, diced
6 green onions, diced
¼ cup chopped
    cilantro
½ cup mayonnaise
    Salt and black
    pepper to taste

Season boiling water with 2 tablespoons lime juice, bay leaf, garlic, salt and cayenne pepper. Add shrimp and cook for 4 to 5 minutes. Drain, peel and devein shrimp. Chill. Combine chilies, tomato, onion and cilantro. Mix 2 tablespoons lime juice and mayonnaise together. Season with salt and pepper. Combine chilled shrimp, vegetable mixture and mayonnaise dressing. Chill for at least 1 hour. Yield: 6 to 8 servings.

Camaron a la Vinagreta

Shrimp with Vinegar

Cook cauliflower and carrots in salted water until crisp-tender. Drain. Combine cooked vegetables, shrimp, green pepper, onion and mushrooms. Combine lemon juice, vinegar, oil, sugar, mustard, cilantro, salt and cayenne pepper. Add marinade to shrimp mixture. Chill, in airtight plastic container, overnight. Drain marinade before serving. Yield: 6 to 8 servings.

- 2 **cups cauliflowerets**
- 4 **large carrots, cut in ½-inch slices**
  Salted water
- 2 **pounds shrimp, cooked, peeled and deveined**
- 1 **large green bell pepper, cut in 1-inch pieces**
- 6 **green onions, diced**
- 1 **pound small mushrooms**
- ½ **cup lemon juice**
- ⅔ **cup cider vinegar**
- 1 **cup olive oil**
- 1½ **tablespoons sugar**
- 1½ **tablespoons Dijon mustard**
- ½ **cup fresh chopped cilantro**
- 1½ **teaspoons salt**
- ⅛ **teaspoon cayenne pepper**

Chile Con Queso

Cheese with Peppers

6 slices bacon, diced
1 medium-sized onion, minced
2 tablespoons minced jalapeño peppers
½ cup minced cilantro
¼ teaspoon oregano
1 large tomato, diced
1¼ teaspoons chili powder
4 cups (16 ounces) grated Cheddar or Velveeta or longhorn cheese
Tostados

Sauté bacon until crisp. Drain excess fat, leaving 1 tablespoon drippings. Sauté onion in bacon drippings for about 1 minute or until tender and transparent. Add jalapeño chilies and cilantro and sauté for 1 minute. Stir in oregano, tomato and chili powder and sauté for 2 minutes. Add cheese and simmer, stirring constantly, until cheese is melted. Serve warm with Tostados (page 43). Yield: 6 to 8 servings.

Variation: To reduce fat grams, omit bacon and prepare skillet with non-stick vegetable spray. Cook onion in 1 tablespoon water. Substitute low or non-fat cheese for regular cheese.

Flautas

Flutes (Crispy Rolled Tacos)

12 corn tortillas
2 cups Tacos Tostados de Pollo chicken mixture (page 67)
1 cup (4 ounces) grated Monterey Jack cheese
Vegetable oil for frying

Warm corn tortillas in microwave or oven to prevent tearing. Place about 2 tablespoons chicken mixture and 1 tablespoon cheese at 1 side of tortilla. Roll tightly and secure with wooden pick. Cook in oil until crisp, turning frequently to cook evenly. Drain on paper towels. Place in warm oven until ready to serve. Serve with guacamole, sour cream or red or green hot sauce. Yield: 6 to 8 servings.

Guacamole

Avocado Dip or Salad

- **4 large ripe avocados, peeled and pitted**
- **2 to 3 tablespoons lemon or lime juice**
- **1 tablespoon minced garlic**
- **¼ cup chopped cilantro**
- **1 large firm tomato, diced**
- **Salt to taste**
- **Tostados**

Using fork or potato masher, mash avocado until coarse consistency. Stir in lemon juice, garlic, cilantro and tomato. Season with salt. Serve with Tostados (page 43). Yield: 4 to 6 servings.

Jalea de Jalapeño

Jalapeño Jelly

- **4 large green bell peppers, seeded**
- **12 large jalapeño peppers, seeded**
- **1½ cups cider vinegar**
- **6½ cups sugar**
- **1 6-ounce bottle fruit pectin**
- **Green food coloring**

Using food processor, chop peppers until fine consistency. Combine peppers, vinegar and sugar in large saucepan. Bring to a boil and cook, stirring constantly, for 10 minutes. Strain mixture through cheesecloth, if desired. Add fruit pectin and boil for 1 minute. Add food coloring, a few drops at a time, until desired color. Pour jelly into sterilized jars and seal according to manufacturer's directions. Serve jelly over block of cream cheese with crackers, as relish with chicken or ham or as glaze for roast pork or ham. Yield: 3 to 5 pints.

Jalapeños Rellenos

Stuffed Jalapeño

**12 to 20 large pickled
jalapeño peppers
Tacos Tostados de
Pollo chicken
mixture (page 67)**
4 eggs, separated
**¼ cup all-purpose
flour**
¼ teaspoon salt
**1 tablespoon water
Canola oil for
frying**

*Wear rubber gloves while handling
jalapeño peppers to prevent irritation.
Slice jalapeños lengthwise, leaving
attached at end and retaining stems if
possible. Carefully scoop out seeds.
Rinse and drain on paper towels.
Spoon well-drained chicken mixture
into jalapeños. Beat egg whites until
stiff. Beat egg yolk with flour, salt and
water. Fold egg yolk mixture into egg
whites. Spoon about 2 tablespoons egg
batter into medium-hot oil in skillet,
place a stuffed jalapeño on egg mixture
and top with 2 tablespoons egg mixture, covering the jalapeño. Cook for 1
to 2 minutes, turn and cook for additional 1 to 2 minutes until golden
brown; do not allow oil to become too
hot. Drain on paper towels and serve
warm. Yield: 8 to 10 servings.*

Pico de Gallo

Roosters Beak (Fresh Chunky Salsa)

**6 jalapeño or serrano
peppers, chopped**
**3 large firm
tomatoes, chopped**
**1 large white onion,
chopped**
**1 cup chopped
cilantro
Juice of 1 lime
Salt to taste**

*Combine peppers, tomatoes, onion,
cilantro and lime juice. Season with
salt. Serve with Tostados (page 43) or
as garnish with beef or chicken fajita
tacos. Yield: 4 to 6 servings.*

Nachos

Tortilla Chips with Melted Cheese

8 corn tortillas, each cut in 4 wedges
Vegetable oil for frying
1 cup (4 ounces) grated Cheddar cheese
1 cup (4 ounces) grated Monterey Jack cheese
32 jalapeño pepper slices

Sauté 4 tortilla wedges at a time in very hot oil in skillet until crisp, pressing lightly to keep wedges flat. Drain on paper towels. Place wedges on baking sheet and cover each with mixture of Cheddar and Monterey Jack cheese. Top each with jalapeño slice. Bake at 350° just until cheese is melted. Serve hot. Yield: 4 to 6 servings.

__Variations:__ Beans: Spread a layer of refried beans (page 51) on tortilla wedges, then add cheese and jalapeños. Chicken: Layer diced chicken mixture from Tacos Tostados de Pollo (page 67) on wedges before adding cheese and jalapeños. Beef: Layer ground beef mixture from Tacos Tostados de Res (page 65) before adding cheese and jalapeños. Super: Spread wedges with refried beans, add chicken or beef mixture and top with cheese. Bake to melt cheese and top with guacamole and jalapeño slice. Serve hot.

Quesadillas

Cheese Filled Tortillas

**12 flour or corn
  tortillas**
 **1 8-ounce can whole
  green chilies**
 **4 cups (16 ounces)
  grated Monterey
  Jack or mozzarella
  cheese
  Vegetable oil for
  frying**

Warm tortillas on hot griddle or in microwave to avoid tearing. Slice chilies in quarters lengthwise. Place chili quarter and 2 to 3 tablespoons cheese in center of each tortilla. Fold and secure with wooden pick. Fry in oil until lightly crisp. Drain on paper towel. Serve warm with hot sauce, sour cream and guacamole as optional toppings. Yield: 6 to 8 servings.

Note: *To reduce fat grams, warm tortillas on medium-hot griddle until cheese is melted; use corn tortillas, low-fat or non-fat cheese and non-fat sour cream, and avoid guacamole.*

Variations: *Meat: Add chicken or beef, leftover from fajitas, with cheese mixture before cooking. Hot: Substitute jalapeño peppers for green chilies. Hotter: Use 1 to 2 tablespoons of Pico de Gallo (page 38).*

Queso Flamadeo

Flamed Cheese

 **1 pound chorizo
  (Mexican sausage)**
 **8 cups (32 ounces)
  grated Monterey
  Jack cheese**
**20 to 25 corn or flour
  tortillas**

Cook sausage according to package directions. Drain all excess fat and crumble. Place sausage in 8x8x2-inch baking dish. Place cheese on sausage. Bake at 350° until cheese is melted. To serve, spoon cheese and sausage mixture into center of warm tortilla. Fold and serve warm. Yield: 8 to 10 servings.

Sauté onion in oil until transparent
and soft. Add mushrooms and chilies,
cooking until tender. Pour vegetables
into 2-quart casserole. Place cheese on
vegetables. Bake at 350° until cheese is
bubbly. To serve, spoon cheese and
vegetable mixture into center of warm
tortilla. Fold and serve warm. Yield: 8
to 10 servings.

Queso Fundido
Melted Cheese

- **1 large onion, thinly sliced**
- **1 tablespoon olive oil**
- **1 cup sliced mushrooms**
- **1 4-ounce can green chilies or fresh Anaheim peppers, thinly sliced**
- **8 cups (32 ounces) shredded Monterey Jack cheese**
- **20 to 25 corn or flour tortillas**

Using blender or food processor,
process onion, garlic and peppers
together. Process tomatillos, cilantro
and cumin; do not over process.
Mixture should be liquid but smooth
and thick. Season with salt. Pour into
saucepan. Bring to a boil over medium
heat, stirring constantly. Let stand
until cool. Serve with Tostados (page
43) or as garnish for other Mexican
dishes. Yield: 8 to 10 servings.

Salsa Verde
Green Sauce

- **1 medium-sized white onion, chopped**
- **1 tablespoon minced garlic**
- **8 to 10 fresh jalapeño or serrano peppers, stemmed or chopped**
- **1 13-ounce can tomatillos, drained**
- **1 cup coarsely chopped cilantro**
- **½ teaspoon cumin**
- **Salt to taste**

Salsas

Hot Sauces

Fresh Sauce

6 to 8 fresh jalapeño
  or serrano peppers,
  stemmed and diced
2 medium-sized ripe
  tomatoes, peeled
  and chopped
  Salt

Grind peppers. Add tomatoes, mashing until smooth consistency. Season with salt. Serve as garnish for Mexican foods. Yield: 4 to 6 servings.

Note: Traditional hot sauce is found as a staple on the Mexican table. Hot sauce comes in many forms: red, green, fresh, cooked. In my home, I use a Mexican stone bowl, a molcajete, and a stone pestle, a tejolote, serving the salsa from the molcajete.
To use a blender, chop chilies to well-ground consistency. Add tomatoes and blend briefly. Season with salt.

Variation: The "hotness" of sauce depends on the number of peppers used.

Cooked Sauce

1 medium-sized white
  onion, chopped
8 to 10 jalapeño or
  serrano peppers,
  stemmed and
  chopped
1 tablespoon minced
  garlic
1 cup coarsely
  chopped cilantro
4 medium to large
  ripe tomatoes or 1
  28-ounce can
  stewed tomatoes
½ teaspoon cumin
  Salt to taste

Using blender or food processor, process onion, peppers and garlic together until finely chopped. Process cilantro, tomatoes and cumin; do not over process. Mixture should be liquid but smooth and thick. Season with salt. Pour into saucepan. Bring to a boil over medium heat, stirring constantly. Let stand until cool. Serve with Tostados (page 43) or as garnish for other Mexican dishes. Yield: 8 to 10 servings.

Taquitos

Little Tacos
  20 corn tortillas
    **2 to 3 cups Carne
      Guisada beef
      mixture (page 53)
      Vegetable oil for
      frying**

Warm tortillas, 6 at a time, in microwave for about 30 seconds or until soft. Fill each tortilla with beef mixture which has been shredded by hand. Roll tortillas and secure with wooden pick. Fry in oil in skillet until crisp. Drain on paper towel. Serve warm with guacamole, sour cream and red or green hot sauce. Yield: 8 to 10 servings.

Tostados

Fried Tortilla Chips

  **12 corn tortillas
      Vegetable oil for
      frying
      Seasoned salt**

Cut each tortilla into 4 to 6 wedges. Sauté in oil, turning to crisp and lightly brown on each side. Drain on paper towel. Season with seasoned salt. Yield: 6 to 8 servings.

__Variation:__ To reduce fat grams, use tongs to dip tortillas in cold water, 1 at a time. Lightly salt each side. Cut into wedges and place in single layer on baking sheet. Bake at 500° for 3 minutes, turn and continue baking for 2 minutes or until golden brown and crisp.

Caldos O Sopas

Soups

1. *Caldo de Pollo — Chicken Soup*
2. *Caldo de Res — Beef Soup*
3. *Sopa de Arroz con Chorizo — Sausage and Rice Soup*
4. *Sopa de Tortilla — Tortilla Soup*

Caldo de Pollo

Chicken Soup

5 pounds chicken, cut up and skin removed

6 cups water

1 medium-sized onion, thickly sliced

1 cup chopped cilantro

2 tablespoons minced garlic

1 teaspoon salt

⅛ teaspoon black pepper

¼ teaspoon cumin

1 16-ounce can tomatoes, cut up

2 cups sliced carrots

4 chicken bouillon cubes

2 16-ounce packages frozen green peas

Combine chicken, water, onion, cilantro, garlic, salt, black pepper and cumin in stock pot. Cook, covered, over medium heat for 1 hour. Add tomatoes, carrots, bouillon and peas. Simmer for 30 minutes or until carrots are tender. Yield: 8 to 10 servings.

Caldo de Res

Beef Soup

3 pounds very lean short ribs
12 cups water
1½ cups 1-inch pieces celery
1 medium-sized onion, chopped
2 to 3 tablespoons minced garlic
Salt to taste
2 large carrots, cut in ½-inch slices
2 large potatoes, cut in 1-inch cubes
2 ears corn, cut in 8 pieces
2 large zucchini, cut in 1-inch pieces
2 cups chopped cilantro
2 16-ounce cans seasoned tomato sauce
2 cups coarsely shredded cabbage

Combine ribs, water, celery, onion, garlic and salt in stock pot. Simmer for 2 hours or until ribs are tender. Add carrots, potatoes, corn, zucchini, cilantro and tomato sauce. Simmer for 15 to 20 minutes. Stir in cabbage and cook for 5 minutes. Season with salt. Yield: 8 to 10 servings.

Sopa de Arroz Con Chorizo

Sausage and Rice Soup

½ **cup shredded cabbage**
½ **cup sliced turnip**
2 **tablespoons butter or margarine**
¾ **cup sweet Italian sausage**
6 **cups chicken broth**
¼ **teaspoon oregano**
¼ **cup regular rice, cooked**

Sauté cabbage and turnips in butter until tender and golden. Transfer to Dutch oven. Sauté sausage, stirring to crumble, until browned. Drain excess fat and add to vegetables. Add broth and oregano to sausage mixture. Bring to a boil, then reduce heat. Add rice and simmer for 30 minutes. Yield: 4 to 6 servings.

Sopa de Tortilla

Tortilla Soup

1 **medium-sized onion, diced**
1 **tablespoon olive oil**
1 **10-ounce can diced tomatoes with chilies**
2 **tablespoons minced garlic**
¼ **cup chopped cilantro**
6 **cups chicken broth**
  Tortillas
  Vegetable oil for frying
  Grated Cheddar or Monterey Jack cheese
  Avocado slices

Sauté onion in oil until tender and transparent. Add tomatoes with chilies, garlic and cilantro. Simmer until tender. Transfer vegetables to stock pot. Add broth. Bring to a boil, reduce heat and simmer for about 30 minutes. Slice tortillas into strips and fry in hot oil until crisp. Drain on paper towels. Place tortilla strips, cheese and avocado slices in individual soup bowls, ladle soup into bowls and serve hot. Yield: 4 to 6 servings.

Vegetables

Vegetables

1. Calabacita Mexicana — Mexican Squash
2. Fideo — Mexican Vermicelli
3. Arroz Mexicana — Mexican Rice
4. Frijoles — Beans
   Frijoles de Olla — Basic Beans from the Pot
   Frijoles Borrachos — Drunk (Cooked with Beer)
   Frijoles Españoles — Spanish
   Frijoles Refritos — Refried
5. Papas Fritas

Calabacita Mexicana

Mexican Squash

1 large onion, thinly sliced
3 tablespoons olive oil
2 tablespoons minced garlic
1 large green bell pepper, cut in strips
1 large red bell pepper, cut in strips
2 medium zucchini, cut in 2-inch strips
2 medium-sized yellow squash, cut in 2-inch strips
1 cup sliced mushrooms
Salt to taste
¼ teaspoon black pepper
2 teaspoons basil

Sauté onion in oil until tender and transparent. Add garlic and sauté for 1 minute. Add green and red peppers, zucchini, squash, mushrooms, salt, black pepper and basil. Cook for about 5 minutes or until vegetables are tender. Yield: 6 to 8 servings.

Variation: To reduce fat grams, use olive oil-flavored non-stick vegetable spray instead of olive oil.

47

Fideo

Mexican Vermicelli

1 8-ounce package
fideo or vermicelli
pasta, broken
2 tablespoons minced
garlic
2 tablespoons canola
or olive oil
1 10½-ounce can
chopped Mexican
stewed tomatoes
2 10-ounce cans
chicken broth
1 cup water
¼ cup chopped
cilantro
Salt to taste
½ teaspoon cumin

Sauté pasta and garlic in oil in 4-quart saucepan until golden brown. Add tomatoes and sauté for about 2 minutes. Stir in broth, water, cilantro, salt and cumin. Bring to a boil, reduce heat and simmer, covered, for about 20 minutes or until pasta is tender. Yield: 8 to 10 servings.

Arroz Mexicano

Mexican Rice

1 cup uncooked long
grain rice
2 tablespoons canola
or olive oil
½ cup chopped green
onion with stems
2 tablespoons minced
garlic
1 cup chopped
tomatoes
2 cups chicken broth
Salt and black
pepper to taste
½ teaspoon cumin

Sauté rice in oil, stirring constantly, until golden brown. Add green onion and garlic and sauté for 1 minute. Add tomatoes and sauté for 1 minute. Add broth, salt, black pepper and cumin. Bring to a boil, stirring occasionally, reduce heat and simmer, tightly covered, for 20 minutes; do not stir. Yield: 4 to 6 servings.

Frijoles

Beans

Always clean pinto beans before soaking them. Once you have cleaned them, put them in a bowl and cover with hot water and let them soak overnight.

I often don't have time to soak beans overnight. You can cover with hot water and boil for 2 minutes. Then take off heat and let stand for 1 hour.

Once beans are ready to cook, put in your cooking pot and cover with water. Add basic ingredients, except salt. Salt has a tendency to make beans hard. I add salt when beans are almost cooked.

Frijoles de Olla

Basic Beans from the Pot

2 cups dried pinto beans
Water
½ onion, coarsely chopped
2 tablespoons minced garlic
2 tablespoons lard, bacon drippings or olive oil
Salt and black pepper to taste

Clean and soak beans. Drain, rinse, place in large saucepan and cover with hot water. Bring to a boil. Add onion, garlic and lard. Simmer, covered, for 4 to 6 hours or until beans are tender, adding water as needed to cover beans. Season with salt and pepper just before serving. Yield: 6 to 8 servings.

Variation: To reduce fat grams, omit lard, bacon drippings or olive oil.

Frijoles Borrachos

Drunk Beans (Cooked with Beer)

1 recipe Basic Beans
1 cup chopped cilantro
1 cup pico de gallo
1 12-ounce can beer, flat

Prepare beans according to basic recipe. After adding salt, add cilantro and cook for 30 minutes. Stir in pico de gallo and beer and simmer for additional 30 minutes. Yield: 6 to 8 servings.

Frijoles Españoles

Spanish Beans

6 slices bacon
1 large onion, sliced
2 medium tomatoes, diced
2 teaspoons chili powder
¼ teaspoon cumin
1 recipe Basic Beans

Sauté bacon until cooked. Drain, reserving 2 tablespoons bacon drippings. Sauté onion in bacon drippings until tender. Add tomatoes and cook until tender. Stir in chili powder and cumin; mixture will resemble roux. Simmer, stirring gently, for 2 minutes. Stir in prepared beans. Simmer for about 1 hour, stirring occasionally. Yield: 6 to 8 servings.

Variation: *To reduce fat grams, omit bacon and sauté onion in pan prepared with non-stick vegetable spray.*

Frijoles Refritos
Refried Beans

4 cups Basic Beans
3 tablespoons lard, bacon drippings or olive oil

Drain broth from beans. Add beans to hot lard in skillet. Mash with potato masher, adding small amount of broth if beans become too thick. Simmer until fat is completely absorbed by beans. Yield: 6 to 8 servings.

Variation: To reduce fat grams, omit lard and use additional broth to keep beans from sticking while frying. Canned beans are available in vegetarian form.
For special flavor, add 1 teaspoon chili powder.
Refried beans may be used in recipes for nachos, bean dip, chalupas and other Mexican dishes.

Papas Fritas
Fried Potatoes

4 slices bacon
4 large potatoes, peeled and sliced
1 large onion, thinly sliced
Salt and black pepper to taste

Sauté bacon in heavy skillet until just crisp. Drain bacon drippings, reserving 2 tablespoons in skillet. Add potatoes and onion to bacon drippings. Season with salt and black pepper. Toss vegetables. Cook, covered, over medium heat, checking and stirring to prevent potatoes from sticking to skillet. When potatoes are tender, remove cover and cook until browned. Yield: 4 to 6 servings.

Variation: To reduce fat grams, omit bacon and substitute non-stick vegetable spray or olive oil for cooking vegetables.

Platos de Cena

Main Dishes

1. *Arroz con Pollo — Chicken and Rice*
2. *Carne Guisada — Mexican Stewed Beef*
3. *Calabacita — Squash with Chicken or Pork*
4. *Chalupas — Little Boats*
5. *Pierna de Cordero — Leg of Lamb*
6. *Chiles Rellenos — Stuffed Peppers*
7. *Carne de Res Ala Mexicana — Mexican Brisket*
8. *Carnitas de Puerco — Pork Roast*
9. *Fajitas — Beef and Chicken Meat Strips*
10. *Tortas Mexicanas — Mexican Sandwiches*
11. *Huachinango Ala Veraeruzana — Red Snapper Veracruz*
12. *Enchiladas — Enchiladas*
    > *Enchiladas de Jaiba — Crab Enchiladas*
    > *Enchiladas de Pollo — Chicken Enchiladas*
    > *Enchiladas Verdes — Green Enchiladas*
    > *Enchiladas de Queso — Cheese Enchiladas*
    > *Enchiladas de Res — Beef Enchiladas*
13. *Tacos - Tacos*
    > *Tacos Suaves de Pollo — Soft Chicken Tacos*
    > *Tacos Tostada de Res — Crispy Beef Tacos*
    > *Tacos Suaves de Res — Soft Beef Tacos*
    > *Salsa de Tomate — Tomato Sauce*
    > *Tacos Tostada de Pollo — Crispy Chicken Tacos*
14. *Tortillas de Harina — Flour Tortilla*
15. *Tortillas de Maiz — Corn Tortilla*

Arroz con Pollo

Chicken and Rice

- **4 pounds chicken, cut up**
- **1 medium-sized onion, chopped**
- **4 tablespoons minced garlic**
  Salt and black pepper to taste
- **2 cups uncooked long grain rice**
- **2 tablespoons canola or olive oil**
- **1 cup chopped ripe tomatoes**
- **½ cup tomato sauce**
- **4 cups chicken broth**
- **½ teaspoon cumin**

Place chicken in Dutch oven. Add onion and garlic. Season with salt and black pepper. Cook, covered, over medium heat until chicken is lightly browned. Sauté rice in oil in skillet until golden brown. Stir in chopped tomatoes. Add tomato sauce, broth and cumin. Season with salt and black pepper. Bring to a boil, then add rice mixture to chicken. Cook, covered, over medium heat until rice is tender and most of liquid is absorbed. Serve with beans, flour or corn tortillas and hot sauces. Yield: 6 to 8 servings.

Carne Guisada

Mexican Stewed Beef

- **2 pounds chuck steak or rump roast, cut into bite-sized pieces**
- **2 tablespoons canola or olive oil**
- **2 tablespoons all-purpose flour**
- **2 tablespoons minced garlic**
- **1 teaspoon cumin**
- **2 cups chicken broth**
  Salt and black pepper to taste
- **1 large green bell pepper, diced**

Sauté beef in oil until beef is browned. Add flour, stirring to thoroughly coat beef and flour begins to brown. Add garlic, cumin and broth. Season with salt and black pepper. Stir in green pepper. Bring to a gentle boil over low heat, stirring occasionally. Simmer for 1 hour or until beef is fork tender but not over cooked. Yield: 6 to 8 servings.

Calabacita

Squash with Chicken or Pork

Chicken

3 **pounds chicken, cut up**
¼ **cup minced garlic**
  Salt and black pepper to taste
1 **large onion, chopped**
4 **cups diced zucchini or tatuma squash**
2 **cups diced ripe tomatoes**
1 **teaspoon cumin**
2 **12-ounce cans shoe peg corn, drained**

Place chicken in Dutch oven. Add garlic and season with salt and black pepper. Saute until chicken is lightly browned. Add onion, squash, tomatoes and cumin. Simmer, covered, for 30 minutes or until squash is tender. Add corn and cook for 10 to 15 minutes or until thoroughly heated. Yield: 4 to 6 servings.

Pork

2 **pounds pork loin chops, cut in bite-sized pieces**
¼ **cup minced garlic**
1 **large onion, chopped**
4 **cups zucchini or tatuma squash**
2 **cups diced ripe tomatoes**
1 **teaspoon cumin**
1 **16-ounce package frozen green peas or shoepeg corn**
  Salt and black pepper to taste

Place pork in Dutch oven. Add garlic and season with salt and black pepper. Sauté until pork is lightly browned. Add onion, squash, tomatoes and cumin. Simmer, covered, for 30 minutes or until squash is tender. Add peas and cook for 10 to 15 minutes or until thoroughly heated. Season with salt and black pepper. Yield: 4 to 6 servings.

Chalupas
Little Boats

Fry tortillas in oil, 1 at a time, pressing with metal spatula to flatten, until tortilla is crisp and golden brown. Drain on paper towel. Spread refried beans on each tortilla and sprinkle with cheese. Place on baking sheet. Bake at 250° just until cheese is melted. Remove from oven. Sprinkle lettuce and tomatoes on cheese. Spoon dollop of guacamole on tomatoes and add hot sauce. Serve with a light dinner or a Mexican rice or fideo on the side. Yield: 4 to 6 servings.

Variation: For a heartier chalupa, add a layer of beef or chicken from taco recipes (pages 65 and 67) on refried beans.

- **12 corn tortillas**
  Canola or olive oil
  for frying
- **4 cups Refried Beans**
  (page 51)
- **2 cups (8 ounces)**
  grated longhorn
  cheese
- **4 cups finely**
  shredded lettuce
- **2 cups sliced ripe**
  tomatoes
- **2 cups guacamole**
  Hot sauce
  (optional)

Pierna de Cordero
Leg of Lamb

Place lamb in roasting pan. Rub lamb with garlic and season with salt and black pepper. Spread tomato paste on lamb. Arrange onion and green pepper slices on lamb and sprinkle with basil. Cover tightly with aluminum foil. Bake at 350° for 2½ to 3 hours or until lamb is tender. Serve with warm flour or corn tortillas. Yield: 8 to 10 servings.

- **4 to 5 pound leg of**
  lamb, fat trimmed
- **3 to 4 tablespoons**
  minced garlic
  Salt and black
  pepper to taste
- **1 6-ounce can tomato**
  paste
- **2 medium-sized**
  onions, sliced
- **2 large green bell**
  peppers, sliced
- **2 tablespoons dried**
  basil

Chiles Rellenos

Stuffed Peppers

12 **California or Anaheim peppers with steams**

2 **cups Chicken Filling (page 67)**

1½ **cups all-purpose flour, divided**

8 **eggs, separated**

2 **tablespoons water**

½ **teaspoon salt**

Vegetable oil for frying

1 **tablespoon olive oil**

1 **medium-sized onion, chopped**

2 **tablespoons minced garlic**

½ **cup chopped cilantro**

1 **16-ounce can tomatoes, chopped**

¼ **teaspoon cumin**

Place peppers on baking sheet. Bake at 350° for about 30 minutes or until skin of peppers begins to puff. Remove carefully from baking sheet and cool with cold water. Remove pepper skins and carefully slit peppers to form pocket. Spoon chicken filling into peppers and fold slit over to enclose stuffing. Gently dredge stuffed peppers in 1 cup flour. Beat egg whites until stiff peaks form. Combine egg yolks, ½ cup flour, 2 tablespoons water and salt, beating well. Fold egg whites into yolk mixture. Spoon ½ cup egg mixture into hot oil in small skillet over medium heat. Place stuffed pepper in center of mounded egg mixture. Spoon additional egg mixture on top of pepper. Cook until egg mixture is set, turn and cook for about 2 minutes or until golden brown. Drain on paper towels. Repeat with remaining peppers and egg mixture. Prepare tomato sauce by sautéing onion and garlic in 1 tablespoon oil until tender. Add cilantro, tomatoes and cumin. Cook until sauce consistency. Serve stuffed peppers with tomato sauce, rice, beans and corn or flour tortillas. Yield: 4 servings.

Carne de Res Ala Mexicana

Mexican Brisket

4 pounds lean beef brisket
4 tablespoons minced garlic
2 envelopes onion soup mix
Salt and black pepper to taste
2 tablespoons crushed oregano
1 teaspoon cumin

Place brisket in large baking dish. Rub brisket with garlic. Sprinkle soup mix on brisket, season lightly with salt and black pepper and sprinkle with oregano and cumin. Cover tightly with aluminum foil. Bake at 350° for 3 to 4 hours or until brisket is tender. Cut in thin slices. Serve with corn or flour tortillas. Garnish with choice of shredded lettuce, diced tomatoes, guacamole, sour cream and hot sauce. Yield: 8 to 10 servings.

Carnitas de Puerco

Pork Roast

4 pounds pork butt roast
Water
4 tablespoons minced garlic
Salt and black pepper to taste
½ teaspoon cumin

Place pork in Dutch oven. Add water to cover. Add garlic and season with salt, black pepper and cumin. Bring to a boil, then reduce heat and simmer, covered, for 3 to 4 hours. Remove pork from pan liquids. Place in baking dish and season with salt and black pepper. Bake at 350° for 1½ to 2 hours. Shred roasted meat with fork. Serve with corn or flour tortillas. Garnish with choice of shredded lettuce, diced tomatoes, guacamole, sour cream and hot sauce. Yield: 8 to 10 servings.

Fajitas

Beef or Chicken Meat Strips

4 pounds skirt steak, trimmed, or 4 pounds chicken breasts
2 large green bell peppers, sliced
2 large onions, sliced
6 tablespoons minced garlic
1 cup olive oil
1 cup red wine
½ cup vinegar
½ cup apple juice
Salt and black pepper to taste
Corn or flour tortillas
Guacamole
Hot sauce
Sour cream

Place steak or chicken, green peppers, onion and garlic in baking dish or plastic container. Combine oil, wine, vinegar, apple juice, salt and black pepper. Pour over steak and vegetables. Marinate overnight. Drain marinade. Grill steak over hot coals or in iron skillet on stove top. Cut in long strips. Sauté onion and green pepper in pan until tender and serve as garnish with steak strips. Serve in tortillas with guacamole, hot sauce and sour cream. Yield: 10 to 12 servings.

Tortas Mexicanas

Mexican Sandwiches

8 to 10 French rolls
2 cups Refried Beans (page 51)
4 cups Mexican Beef (page 57) or Pork Roast (page 57)
Guacamole
Hot sauce

Heat rolls in oven at 350° until warm and crusty. Split lengthwise, leaving 1 side intact. Spread beans on roll, fill with meat mixture and garnish with guacamole and hot sauce. Yield: 8 to 10 servings.

Huachinango Ala Veraeruzana

Red Snapper Veracruz

Sauté onion in 2 tablespoons oil in saucepan until tender. Add garlic and sauté for 1 minute. Add tomatoes, olives and cilantro. Season with salt and black pepper. Add water and bring to a low boil, stirring occasionally, and simmer for 10 to 12 minutes. Dip filets in egg and dredge with flour. Fry in oil until golden brown on both sides. Place on serving dish. Pour tomato sauce over filets. Serve immediately. Yield: 6 to 8 servings.

- **1 medium-sized onion, thinly sliced**
- **2 tablespoons olive oil**
- **¼ cup minced garlic**
- **6 tomatoes, diced**
- **1 cup pimiento-stuffed Spanish green olives, sliced**
- **½ cup chopped cilantro**
- **Salt and black pepper to taste**
- **½ cup water**
- **2 pounds red snapper filets**
- **2 eggs, lightly beaten**
- **1 cup all-purpose flour**
- **Canola or olive oil for frying**

Enchiladas

Basic Red Sauce

Heat oil in saucepan. Add flour and cook, stirring constantly, until flour is browned. Add chili powder and continue cooking. Add tomato sauce. Gradually add broth, stirring constantly until smooth. Season with salt. Yield: 3 cups.

- **3 tablespoons canola or olive oil**
- **2 tablespoons all-purpose flour**
- **3 to 4 tablespoons chili powder**
- **½ cup tomato sauce**
- **2 cups chicken broth**
- **Salt to taste**

Enchiladas de Jaiba

Crab Enchiladas

¼ **cup butter**
¼ **cup all-purpose flour**
1 **10¾-ounce can chicken broth**
¾ **cup water**
2 **cups sour cream**
1 **4-ounce can green chilies, chopped**
12 **white or red corn tortillas**
  Canola or olive oil for frying
1 **pound cooked fresh crab, drained and flaked**
2 **cups (8 ounces) grated Monterey Jack cheese, divided**

Melt butter in saucepan over low heat. Add flour, stirring until smooth, and cook for 1 minute. Gradually add broth and water, stirring and cooking until thickened and bubbly. Stir in sour cream and chilies. Using tongs to handle, fry tortillas, 1 at a time, in hot oil just until limp. Drain on paper towels. Place ⅓ of sauce in bottom of 13x9x2-inch baking dish. Place portion of crab and 2 tablespoons cheese on lower ½ of each tortilla and roll tightly. Place on sauce in baking dish, seam side down. Pour remaining sauce over tortilla rolls. Bake at 425° for 20 minutes. Sprinkle with remaining cheese and bake until melted. Yield: 4 to 6 servings.

Variation: To reduce fat grams, avoid frying tortillas in oil. Heat in kitchen towel in microwave for 45 to 60 seconds or until soft. Substitute low-fat or fat-free cheese for regular cheese.

Enchiladas de Pollo

Chicken Enchiladas

Using tongs to handle, fry tortillas in oil, 1 at a time, just until soft. Drain on paper towel. Dip each tortilla in red sauce briefly and place on plate. Place 2 tablespoons cheese, chicken mixture and onion on lower ½ of each tortilla and roll tightly. Place in 13x9x2-inch baking dish, seam side down. Pour remaining sauce over tortilla rolls and sprinkle with remaining cheese and onion. Bake at 425° for 15 to 20 minutes or until cheese is melted. Yield: 4 to 6 servings.

Variation: To reduce fat grams, avoid frying tortillas in oil. Heat in kitchen towel in microwave for 45 to 60 seconds or until soft. Substitute low-fat or fat-free cheese for regular cheese.

12 white or red corn tortillas
Canola or olive oil for frying
Basic Red Sauce (page 59)
3 cups (12 ounces) grated Monterey Jack cheese
Chicken Filling (page 67)
4 green onions with tops, minced

Enchiladas Verdes

Green Chicken Enchiladas

2 4-ounce cans green chilies
2 13-ounce cans tomatillo sauce
½ cup coarsely chopped cilantro
1½ cups whipping cream
1 egg
Salt to taste
12 to 16 white or red corn tortillas
Canola or olive oil for frying
2 cups Chicken Filling (page 67)
3 cups (12 ounces) grated Monterey Jack cheese, divided
6 green onions with tops, minced
Guacamole
Sour cream

Combine chilies, tomatillo sauce, cilantro, cream and egg in blender container. Process until very smooth. Season with salt. Using tongs to handle, fry tortillas, 1 at a time, in oil, just until soft. Drain on paper towel. Combine chicken mixture, 2 cups cheese and onion. Place small amount on lower ½ of each tortilla and roll tightly. Place, seam side down, in 13x9x2-inch baking dish. Pour cream sauce over enchiladas. Sprinkle with 1 cup cheese. Bake at 350° for 15 to 20 minutes or until cheese is melted and bubbly. Garnish with guacamole and sour cream. Yield: 6 to 8 servings.

Variation: To reduce fat grams, avoid frying tortillas in oil. Heat in kitchen towel in microwave for 45 to 60 seconds or until soft. Substitute low-fat or fat-free cheese for regular cheese.

Enchiladas de Queso

Cheese Enchiladas

Using tongs to handle, fry tortillas, 1 at a time, in oil just until soft. Drain on paper towel. Dip tortillas, 1 at a time, in red sauce briefly and place on plate. Combine 2½ cups longhorn cheese, 2½ cups Monterey Jack cheese and onion. Place small amount of cheese mixture on lower ½ of each tortilla and roll tightly. Place, seam side down, in 13x9x2-inch baking dish. Pour red sauce over tortilla rolls and sprinkle with remaining cheese. Bake at 350° for 15 to 20 minutes or until cheese is melted. Yield: 4 to 6 servings.

Variation: To reduce fat grams, avoid frying tortillas in oil. Heat in kitchen towel in microwave for 45 to 60 seconds or until soft. Substitute low-fat or fat-free cheese for regular cheese.

12 **white or red corn tortillas**
   Canola or olive oil for frying
   Basic Red Sauce (page 59)
3 **cups (12 ounces) grated longhorn cheese, divided**
3 **cups (12 ounces) grated Monterey Jack cheese, divided**
6 **green onions with tops, minced**

Enchiladas de Res

Beef Enchiladas

12 white or red corn tortillas
Canola or olive oil for frying
Basic Red Sauce (page 59)
3 cups (12 ounces) grated longhorn cheese, divided
Beef Filling (page 65)
1 medium-sized onion, minced, divided

Using tongs to handle, fry tortillas, 1 at a time, in oil just until soft. Drain on paper towel. Dip tortillas, 1 at a time, in red sauce briefly and place on plate. Place 3 tablespoons cheese, portion of beef mixture and 1 teaspoon onion on lower ½ of each tortilla and roll tightly. Place, seam side down, in 13x9x2-inch baking dish. Pour red sauce over tortilla rolls and sprinkle with remaining cheese and onion. Bake at 350° for 15 to 20 minutes or until cheese is melted. Yield: 4 to 6 servings.

Variation: To reduce fat grams, avoid frying tortillas in oil. Heat in kitchen towel in microwave for 45 to 60 seconds or until soft. Substitute low-fat or fat-free cheese for regular cheese.

Tacos Suaves de Pollo

Soft Chicken Tacos

12 corn tortillas
Canola or olive oil
Chicken Filling (page 67)
Grated longhorn cheese

Dip tortillas in medium-hot oil, immediately remove and stack on plate. Place ¼ cup chicken mixture on lower end of tortilla and roll. Place in 13x9x2-inch baking dish. Combine 1 cup chicken mixture and reserved broth in saucepan. Simmer for 5 minutes. Pour sauce over tortilla rolls and sprinkle with cheese. Bake at 350° until cheese is melted. Yield: 6 to 8 servings.

Tacos Tostados de Res

Crispy Beef Tacos

Filling
- **2 pounds lean ground chuck**
- **1 medium-sized onion, diced**
- **2 tablespoons minced garlic**
- **2 medium tomatoes, diced**
- **Salt and black pepper to taste**
- **1 teaspoon ground cumin**

Tacos
- **12 corn tortillas or prepared taco shells**
- **Canola or olive oil for frying**
- **Beef Filling**
- **Shredded lettuce**
- **Diced tomatoes**
- **Grated longhorn cheese**
- **Hot sauce**

Sauté beef in large skillet or Dutch oven, stirring to crumble, until browned. Add onion and garlic. Sauté until onion is tender. Drain excess fat. Add tomatoes, salt, black pepper and cumin. Simmer, covered, for about 25 minutes.

Fry tortillas, 1 at a time, in medium hot oil. Using metal spatula, fold to semi-circle shape. When 1 side is crisp, turn to fry other, keeping tortilla open as it crisps. Drain on paper towel. Keep warm in oven until ready to fill. Spoon portion of beef mixture into shell and top with lettuce, tomatoes, cheese and hot sauce. Yield: 6 to 8 servings.

Tacos Suaves de Res

Soft Beef Tacos

Salsa de Tomate
Tomato Sauce

1 **medium-sized onion, sliced** 2 **tablespoons olive oil** ½ **cup chopped cilantro** 1 **tablespoon minced garlic** 1 **16-ounce can stewed tomatoes, chopped** **Salt to taste**	*Sauté onion in oil until tender. Add cilantro and garlic. Sauté for 2 minutes over low heat. Add tomatoes and season with salt. Simmer for 10 minutes or until tomatoes are very tender. Yield: 2 cups sauce.*

Tacos

12 **corn tortillas** **Canola or olive oil** **Beef Filling (page 65)** **Tomato sauce** **Grated longhorn cheese**	*Dip tortillas in medium-hot oil, immediately remove and stack on plate. Place ¼ cup beef mixture on lower end of tortilla and roll. Place in 13x9x2-inch baking dish. Pour tomato sauce over tortilla rolls and sprinkle with cheese. Bake at 350° until cheese is melted. Yield: 6 to 8 servings.*

Place chicken in large saucepan. Add water to cover, garlic, salt and black pepper. Bring to a boil, reduce heat and simmer, covered, until chicken is tender. Remove chicken, reserving broth. Dice chicken. Sauté onion in oil until tender. Add tomatoes, chicken and cumin. Simmer while preparing taco shells, adding small amount of broth if chicken is too dry.

Fry tortillas, 1 at a time, in medium hot oil. Using metal spatula, fold to semi-circle shape. When 1 side is crisp, turn to fry other, keeping tortilla open as it crisps. Drain on paper towel. Keep warm in oven until ready to fill. Spoon portion of chicken mixture into shell and top with lettuce, tomatoes, cheese and hot sauce. Yield: 6 to 8 servings.

Tacos Tostados de Pollo

Crispy Chicken Tacos

Chicken Filling
- **2 pounds chicken breasts, boned**
- **Water**
- **2 tablespoons minced garlic**
- **Salt and black pepper to taste**
- **1 large onion, diced**
- **2 tablespoons canola or olive oil**
- **2 medium-sized tomatoes, diced, or 1 15-ounce can seasoned tomato sauce**
- **1 teaspoon cumin**

Tacos
- **12 corn tortillas or prepared taco shells**
- **Canola or olive oil for frying**
- **Chicken Filling**
- **Shredded lettuce**
- **Diced tomatoes**
- **Grated longhorn cheese**
- **Hot sauce**

Tortillas de Harina

Flour Tortilla

2 **cups all-purpose
flour**
¼ **teaspoon baking
powder**
½ **teaspoon salt**
¼ **cup vegetable
shortening**
½ **cup warm water
All-purpose flour**

Combine flour, baking powder and salt. Add shortening, mixing until well blended. Add water and mix to form soft dough. Knead, then roll into ball and coat with flour. Place in bowl, cover with dry towel and let stand. Preheat ungreased griddle or iron skillet on medium-high heat. Shape dough into 8 to 10 balls. On floured surface, roll each as thinly as possible, retaining circle shape. Cook on griddle, turning when bubbles form on top and underside begins to brown, and lightly brown on second side. Serve immediately as bread with any Mexican dish. Yield: 8 to 10 servings.

Tortillas de Maiz

Corn Tortilla

2 **cups masa harina**
1⅓ **cups warm water**

Combine masa harina and warm water, blending well. Using slightly wet hands, shape into 10 to 12 balls. Press with hands to flatten into circle shape. Cook on medium-hot griddle, turning to lightly brown on both sides. Serve immediately with any Mexican dish. Yield: 10 to 12 servings.

Note: *Most grocery stores carry flour and corn tortillas. I recommend you buy them to make your Mexican dishes easier to prepare. I definitely recommend using prepared corn tortillas for taco and enchilada dishes.*

Postres

Desserts

1. *Ensalada de Fruta Tropical — Tropical Fresh Fruit Salad*
2. *Flan — Mexican Custard*
3. *Bola de Caramelo — Caramel Ball*
4. *Pastel de Queso — Cheesecake*
5. *Pastel de Cajeta — Praline and Cream Pie*
6. *Buñuelos — Fried Flat Bread*
7. *Capirotada Con Queso — Bread Pudding with Cheese*

Ensalada de Fruta Tropical

Tropical Fresh Fruit Salad

3 kiwi, peeled and cut in thick slices
1 jar mango, drained
1 pint strawberries, thickly sliced
1 pineapple, peeled, sliced and cut in bite-sized chunks
1 tablespoon fruit freshener
2 tablespoons sugar
Mint

Combine kiwi, mango, strawberries, pineapple, fruit freshener and sugar, tossing gently to mix. Spoon into individual dessert dishes and garnish with mint leaves. Chill until ready to serve. Salad may be served prior to meal or as light dessert. Yield: 6 to 8 servings.

Variations: *Fresh mango may be substituted for prepared mango, raspberries for strawberries and canned pineapple for fresh pineapple. Serve salad with flan or on angel food or sponge cake slice with scoop of fat-free ice cream.*

Flan

Mexican Custard

This is not a traditional flan recipe but I have created it with a little this and that and it is truly fool proof. It is a classic Mexican dessert. The cooking method is called bono de Maria.

- **½ cup caramel topping, warmed**
- **1 14-ounce can sweetened condensed milk**
- **6 eggs**
- **1 tablespoon vanilla**
- **2 teaspoons nutmeg**
- **1 cup half and half**
- **1 cup milk**

Fill 13x9x2-inch baking dish ½ full with water and place in oven at 350°. Pour warm caramel topping into 3-quart soufflé dish and set aside. Combine condensed milk, eggs, vanilla, nutmeg, half and half and milk in container of blender or food processor. Process until well blended. Pour milk mixture carefully into soufflé dish on caramel layer. Place soufflé dish in water in baking dish. Bake for 30 minutes. To check for doneness, gently shake soufflé dish; flan should be consistency of firm gelatin. Continue baking as necessary until flan is firm and wooden pick inserted near center will come out clean. Surface will be golden brown. Remove from oven and let stand until cool. Using knife tip, loosen edge of flan from soufflé dish and invert on serving dish. Scoop melted caramel over flan. Cut into slices to serve. Yield: 10 to 12 servings.

Bola de Caramelo

Caramel Ball

- **2 cups vanilla ice cream, softened**
- **2 cups butterscotch or caramel topping, warmed**
- **1 cup chopped pecans**
- **½ cup chocolate fudge sauce, warmed**

Shape ice cream into ball. Refreeze until firm. Roll in bowl of butterscotch topping, then in pecans. Place on wax paper-lined plate. Refreeze until ready to serve. Pour warm chocolate sauce over ball. Serve as dessert for casual dinners. Yield: 2 to 4 servings.

Pastel de Queso

Cheesecake

Crust
  ¾ **cup graham
    cracker crumbs**
  ¼ **cup sugar**
  ¼ **cup butter**
  ½ **cup chopped pecans**
  ½ **teaspoon cinnamon**

Filling
  3 **8-ounce packages
    cream cheese,
    softened**
1½ **cups sugar**
  ⅛ **teaspoon salt**
  4 **eggs**
  1 **tablespoon vanilla**

Topping
  2 **cups sour cream**
  ¼ **cup sugar**
  2 **teaspoons vanilla**

Combine crumbs, sugar, butter, pecans and cinnamon, mixing thoroughly. Press crumb mixture into bottom of springform pan.

Combine cream cheese, sugar, salt, eggs and vanilla. Using electric mixer, beat until smooth. Pour batter on crust in springform pan. Bake at 375° for 25 minutes. Remove from oven and increase oven to 475°. Spread topping on partially baked batter and continue baking for 5 minutes. Yield: 10 to 12 servings.

Combine sour cream, sugar and vanilla, beating until smooth. Spread on partially baked cheesecake.

Variations: Serve with additional topping of fresh strawberries or blueberries, cherry pie filling, melted caramel with chopped pecans or Fresh Tropical Fruit Salad (page 69).

Pastel de Cajeta

Praline and Cream Pie

1⅓ **cups evaporated milk**

5 **eggs**

⅓ **cup plus 1 tablespoon butter, melted**

1 **cup sugar**

1 **cup firmly-packed brown sugar**

¼ **cup all-purpose flour**

2 **teaspoons vanilla**

1⅔ **cups chopped pecans**

1 **unbaked 10-inch pastry shell**
  Vanilla ice cream

Combine milk, eggs, butter, sugar, brown sugar, flour and vanilla in blender container. Process until smooth. Add pecans. Pour egg mixture into pastry shell. Bake at 350° for 35 to 40 minutes. Serve pie with scoop of vanilla ice cream. Yield: 8 to 10 servings.

Buñuelos

Fried Flat Bread

Combine flour, 4 teaspoons sugar, baking powder and salt. Combine eggs and milk, beating well. Add egg liquid to dry ingredients, stirring until smooth. Place dough on floured surface and knead, adding additional flour, until very smooth. Divide into 16 balls, place in bowl, cover with towel and let stand for 15 to 20 minutes. Combine 1 cup sugar and cinnamon. Roll balls to paper thickness, retaining circle shape. Carefully fry circles, 1 at a time, in medium hot oil, until golden brown. Drain on paper towel. Immediately sprinkle with sugar mixture. Serve as light dessert or snack with Mexican Hot Chocolate (page 76). Yield: 1¼ dozen.

- 2½ **cups all-purpose flour**
- 4 **teaspoons sugar**
- ½ **teaspoon baking powder**
- ½ **teaspoon salt**
- 2 **eggs**
- ½ **cup milk**
  All-purpose flour
- 1 **cup sugar**
- 1 **teaspoon cinnamon**
  Canola oil for frying

Capirotada Con Queso

Bread Pudding with Cheese

Bread Pudding

- ¾ **cup sugar**
- ¾ **cup hot water**
- ¼ **cup butter**
- 1 **teaspoon cinnamon**
- ½ **teaspoon nutmeg**
- 1½ **cups milk**
- 3 **eggs**
- 24 **day-old cinnamon rolls**
- ½ **cup chopped pecans**
- ⅔ **cup golden raisins**
- 1 **21-ounce can apple pie filling**
- 2 **cups (8 ounces) grated Monterey Jack cheese**

Melt sugar in saucepan, stirring frequently to avoid burning. Add hot water and butter to sugar, mixing well. Remove from heat. Stir in cinnamon and nutmeg. Let stand until cool. Combine milk and eggs, beating well. Break cinnamon rolls into bite size pieces and place in mixing bowl. Add pecans, raisins, pie filling and cheese, mixing lightly. Combine cooled sugar water mixture with egg mixture. Pour liquid over cinnamon roll mixture. Spread in buttered 13x9x2-inch baking dish. Bake at 350° 30 minutes until golden brown. Serve hot with custard sauce. Yield: 8 to 10 servings.

Custard Sauce

- ¾ **cup sugar**
- 2 **teaspoons cornstarch**
- ¾ **cup evaporated milk**
- ½ **cup water**
- 2 **egg yolks, beaten**
- 1 **teaspoon vanilla**
- ½ **teaspoon butter extract**

Combine sugar and cornstarch in small saucepan. Gradually add milk, water and egg yolks. Bring to a low boil over medium-low heat, stirring constantly. Add vanilla and butter extract, mixing well. Serve warm over warm bread pudding.

Bebidos

Beverages

1. *Te de Monzana y Conela — Apple Cinnamon Tea*
2. *Piña Colada — Pineapple Coconut Punch*
3. *Chocolate Mexicano — Mexican Chocolate*

Te de Monzana y Canela

Apple Cinnamon Tea

4 family-size tea bags
2 cinnamon sticks
1 cup sugar
1 46-ounce can apple juice

Brew tea according to package directions, adding cinnamon sticks. Stir in sugar. Bring to a boil, reduce heat and simmer for about 15 minutes. Combine sweetened tea and apple juice, adjusting sugar or tea strength to preference. Serve over ice cubes and as beverage for traditional Mexican meal. Yield: 12 to 16 servings.

Piña Colada

Pineapple Coconut Punch

1 15-ounce can pineapple chunks in syrup
1 can Coco Lopez cream of coconut
1 46-ounce can pineapple juice
4 12-ounce bottles ginger ale

Place pineapple with syrup and cream of coconut in blender container. Process until smooth. Freeze overnight. Scoop into individual serving glasses. Add equal amounts of pineapple juice and ginger ale. Frozen mixture may be placed in punch bowl and juice and ginger ale added. Serve in punch cups. Yield: 15 to 20 servings.

Chocolate Mexicano

Mexican Chocolate

4 3-ounce semi-sweet chocolate bars
½ cup sugar
2 teaspoons cinnamon
1 teaspoon vanilla
6 cups milk

Combine chocolate, sugar, cinnamon, vanilla and milk in saucepan. Bring to a boil, beat and bring to a boil again. Serve with coffee cake or buñuelos. Yield: 8 to 10 servings.

IN THE BEGINNING

In
the beginning
God created the heavens
and the earth...
Then God said,
"I give you every seed
bearing plant on the
face of the earth
and every tree that has
fruit with seed in it.
This will be yours for food."
GENESIS 1.1, 29

APPETIZERS & BEVERAGES

Vegetable Dip

1 to 2 tablespoons
sugar
2 tablespoons vinegar
2 eggs
1 tablespoon melted
butter
1 8-ounce package
cream cheese
⅔ cup minced green
bell pepper
⅓ cup grated onion
2 tablespoons
chopped pimiento
¼ teaspoon hot sauce
⅛ teaspoon salt

Combine sugar, vinegar and eggs in top of double broiler. Cook over medium-boiling water until thickened. Remove from heat. Stir in butter, cream cheese, green pepper, onion, pimiento, hot sauce and salt, mixing until cream cheese is smooth. Chill. Serve with fresh vegetables, cut for dipping. Yield: 2 cups.

Fresh Vegetable Dip

2 cups mayonnaise
1 cup sour cream
2 tablespoons
seasoned salt
2 tablespoons parsley
flakes
2 tablespoons dried
minced onion
2 teaspoons dill weed

Combine mayonnaise, sour cream, seasoned salt, parsley, onion and dill weed, mixing thoroughly. Chill. Serve with fresh vegetables, cut for dipping. Yield: 3 cups.

Tzatziki

(Cucumber and Yogurt Salad)

- **2 medium cucumbers, peeled, seeded and coarsely grated**
- **1 cup sour cream**
- **1 cup low-fat plain yogurt**
- **1 tablespoon olive oil**
- **½ teaspoon salt**
  Black pepper to taste
- **2 medium-sized cloves garlic, crushed**

Combine cucumber, sour cream, yogurt, oil, salt, pepper and garlic, mixing thoroughly. Chill, tightly covered, until very cold. Serve with fresh vegetables, cut for dipping, or cracker rounds. Yield: 4 to 5 cups.

Three Cheese Bean Dip

- **1 cup sour cream**
- **1 8-ounce package cream cheese, softened**
- **1 16-ounce can refried beans**
- **½ cup picante sauce**
- **2 teaspoons chili powder**
- **½ teaspoon cumin**
- **1 cup (4 ounces) shredded Cheddar cheese**
- **1 cup (4 ounces) shredded Monterey Jack cheese**

Combine sour cream, cream cheese, beans, picante sauce, chili powder and cumin, mixing thoroughly. Spread ½ of mixture in 8x8x2-inch baking dish. Sprinkle with ½ of Cheddar cheese and ½ of Monterey Jack cheese. Repeat bean mixture and cheese layers. Bake at 350° for 20 minutes or until thoroughly heated. Serve with tortilla chips. Yield: 5 cups.

Delicious Taco Dip

1 8-ounce package
   cream cheese,
   softened
1 16-ounce can chili
   without beans
1 4-ounce can green
   chilies, drained
   and chopped, or ½
   cup chopped fresh
   chilies
1 4-ounce can black
   olives, drained and
   chopped
½ cup chopped green
   onion
2 cups (8 ounces)
   shredded Monterey
   Jack cheese

In order listed, layer ingredients in 9x9x2-inch baking pan: cream cheese, chili, green chilies, olives, onion and cheese. Bake at 350° for 20 minutes. Serve with tortilla chips. Yield: 5 cups.

Hot Sausage and Cheese Dip

1 pound hot bulk
   pork sausage
1 pound ground beef
1 onion, chopped
1 4-ounce can
   mushrooms,
   drained and
   chopped
1 10¾-ounce can
   cream of mushroom
   soup, undiluted
1 32-ounce package
   pasteurized process
   cheese spread,
   cubed

Sauté sausage, beef and onion until meat is browned and onion is tender. Drain excess fat. Add mushrooms, soup and cheese to meat mixture. Cook over low heat until cheese is melted. Serve hot with tortilla chips. Yield: 6 to 7 cups.

Seven Layer Fiesta Dip

Spread refried beans on large round
serving plate. Mix avocados with
lemon juice and spread mixture on
bean layer. Combine sour cream,
mayonnaise and seasoning mix; spread
mixture on avocado layer. In order
listed, add layers of green onion,
tomatoes, olives and cheese. Serve with
tortilla chips. Yield: 10 cups.

1½ 16-ounce cans
refried beans

6 ripe avocados,
peeled and mashed

2 tablespoons lemon
juice

1 cup low-fat sour
cream

2 tablespoons
mayonnaise

1 1¼-ounce envelope
taco seasoning mix

1 bunch green onions,
chopped

2 or 3 tomatoes,
chopped

1 4-ounce can black
olives, drained and
sliced

2 cups (8 ounces)
shredded Cheddar
cheese

Wagon Wheel Dip

Sauté beef until browned, stirring to
crumble. Drain excess fat. Add taco
seasoning to beef. In 12x8x2-inch
baking dish, layer ingredients in order
listed: beans, ½ of picante sauce, 2
cups cheese, beef mixture, ½ of picante
sauce and 2 cups cheese. Bake at 350°
for 20 to 30 minutes or until cheese is
melted. Yield: 8 cups.

1½ pounds lean ground
beef

1 1¼-ounce envelope
taco seasoning mix

1 16-ounce can
refried beans

1 16-ounce jar
picante sauce

4 cups (16 ounces)
grated Cheddar
cheese

Fruit Dip

1 3-ounce package
   cream cheese,
   softened
½ cup sour cream
1 teaspoon grated
   lemon peel
1 tablespoon
   reconstituted lemon
   juice
½ cup strawberry
   preserves

Using electric mixer, beat cream cheese until smooth. Add sour cream, lemon peel, juice and preserves, mixing thoroughly. Chill overnight before serving with fresh fruit cut for dipping. Yield: 1½ cups.

Cheese Crab Spread

1 6-ounce can crab
   meat, drained
½ cup butter, softened
   Garlic salt to taste
1 3-ounce jar
   pasteurized process
   Cheddar cheese
   spread
1½ tablespoons
   mayonnaise
3 or 4 English
   muffins, split

Combine crab meat, butter, garlic salt, cheese and mayonnaise, blending thoroughly. Spread mixture on split English muffin halves. Broil until bubbly and golden brown. Yield: 6 to 8 servings.

Note: Mushroom caps may be stuffed with crab mixture. Bake at 350° for 25 to 30 minutes.

Salmon Dip

3 6-ounce cans salmon, drained, skin and bone removed
1 8-ounce package cream cheese, softened
⅛ teaspoon salt
2 teaspoons garlic powder
2 tablespoons Worcestershire sauce
½ cup chopped green bell pepper
½ cup chopped red bell pepper
2 fresh cayenne peppers

Combine salmon, cream cheese, salt, garlic powder and Worcestershire sauce in food processor container. Process until smooth. Add bell peppers and cayenne peppers and process briefly. Serve with chips or crackers. Yield: 3 cups.

Variation: Deviled ham may be substituted for salmon.

Pashka

4 8-ounce packages cream cheese, softened
1 cup butter, softened
2 cups powdered sugar
3 egg yolks
2 teaspoons vanilla
Grated lemon peel
1 cup slivered almonds

Combine cream cheese and butter, beating until smooth. Add powdered sugar, egg yolks, vanilla and lemon peel, mixing until smooth. Fold in almonds. Pour mixture into 7-cup mold lined with dampened cheesecloth. Chill or freeze overnight; if frozen, let stand to thaw before serving. Invert mold to remove and serve with fresh fruit such as apples or strawberries. Yield: 7 cups.

Shrimp Pâté

1½ pounds bay shrimp,
  cooked, shelled and
  deveined
¼ cup minced onion
½ cup butter, melted
3 tablespoons lemon
  juice
⅔ cup mayonnaise
1 tablespoon
  prepared
  horseradish
1 teaspoon salt
¼ teaspoon white
  pepper
5 dashes
  Worcestershire
  sauce
4 dashes hot pepper
  sauce
  Parsley for garnish

Reserving a few shrimp for garnish, combine remaining shrimp, onion, butter, lemon juice, mayonnaise, horseradish, salt, white pepper, Worcestershire sauce and hot pepper sauce in blender or food processor container. Process until stiff paste forms. Pack shrimp mixture into 3-cup mold. Chill for 4 to 5 hours or until firm. Unmold on serving plate. Garnish with parsley and reserved shrimp. Serve with wheat crackers and cocktail sauce. Yield: 3 cups.

Manhattan Meatballs

1 pound ground pork
1 pound ground veal
2 cups soft bread
  crumbs
½ cup chopped onion
2 tablespoons
  chopped parsley
2 eggs
2 teaspoons salt
2 tablespoons
  margarine
1 10-ounce jar apricot
  preserves
½ cup barbecue sauce

Combine pork, veal, breadcrumbs, onion, parsley, eggs and salt, mixing lightly but thoroughly. Shape mixture into bite-sized meatballs. Sauté in margarine, turning to brown evenly. Place in 2-quart casserole. Combine preserves and barbecue sauce. Pour mixture over meatballs. Bake at 350° for 30 minutes. Yield: 4 to 6 dozen.

Fried Avocados

Combine salt, black pepper, garlic powder and paprika. Set aside. Combine 1½ cups flour, seasoned salt, chili powder and cumin. Set aside. Combine buttermilk, egg, oil, water and ½ cup flour, blending until smooth. Set aside, at room temperature, for at least 30 minutes. About 30 minutes before cooking, cut avocados into wedges and sprinkle with lemon juice. Pour peanut oil to 3-inch depth in heavy pan and heat to 375°. Lightly dust avocado slices with seasoned salt, dip in batter, dredge slices in seasoned flour and dip again in batter. Deep fry, 2 at a time, for 30 to 45 seconds or until golden brown. Drain on paper towel. Serve immediately with fresh salsa. Yield: 12 to 16 servings.

¼ **cup salt**
1 **tablespoon black pepper**
½ **teaspoon garlic powder**
1 **teaspoon paprika**
2 **cups all-purpose flour, divided**
⅛ **teaspoon seasoned salt**
½ **teaspoon chili powder**
2 **teaspoons ground cumin**
1 **cup buttermilk**
1 **egg, beaten**
2 **tablespoons vegetable oil**
½ **cup water**
3 **medium-ripe avocados**
   Lemon juice
   Peanut oil for deep frying

Egg Rolls

1 medium head
   cabbage, shredded
1 or 2 small carrots,
   shredded
2 or 3 green onions,
   minced
   Canola or safflower
   oil
¼ cup soy sauce
1 6-ounce can
   chicken, crab meat
   or salad shrimp,
   drained
   Salt and black
   pepper to taste
1 15-count package
   egg roll wrappers

Stir fry cabbage, carrots and onion in 2 tablespoons oil and soy sauce for 1 minute. Stir in meat and season with salt and pepper. Stir fry for 1 minute, remove from wok or skillet and set aside. Heat 2 cups oil in separate skillet. Spoon 2 to 3 tablespoons vegetable mixture on each egg roll wrapper, fold sides and roll diagonally to enclose filling, brushing edges with water to seal. Fry in hot oil, turning with tongs, until golden brown. Remove and drain on paper towel. Yield: 12 to 15.

Bread Pot Fondue

1 9-inch round loaf of bread
2 cups (8 ounces) shredded Cheddar cheese
2 3-ounce packages cream cheese, softened
1½ cups sour cream
1 cup diced cooked ham
½ cup chopped green onion
1 3-ounce can whole mild or hot green chilies, drained and chopped
1 teaspoon Worcestershire sauce
2 tablespoons vegetable oil
1 tablespoon butter, melted

Cut a slice from top of loaf, reserving slice. Using paring knife, hollow inside of loaf, leaving a ½-inch shell. Cut bread in 1-inch cubes and set aside. Combine Cheddar cheese, cream cheese and sour cream. Stir in ham, onion, chilies and Worcestershire sauce. Spoon filling into bread shell. Cover with reserved slice, tightly wrap in several sheets of heavy-duty aluminum foil and place on baking sheet. Bake at 350° for 1 hour and 10 minutes or until cheese filling is melted and thoroughly heated. Combine bread cubes, vegetable oil and butter, tossing to coat. Place cubes on baking sheet. Bake at 350°, turning occasionally, for 10 to 15 minutes or until golden brown. To serve, remove top slice and stir filling. Serve with bread cubes and assorted fresh vegetables, cut for dipping. Yield: 5 cups.

Vegetable Pizza

2 8-count packages
   refrigerated
   crescent roll dough
2 8-ounce packages
   cream cheese,
   softened
1 cup mayonnaise
1 envelope ranch-
   style salad dressing
   mix
1 cup broccoli
   flowerets
1 cup cauliflower
   flowerets
1 cup chopped green
   pepper
1 cup chopped
   tomatoes
½ cup sliced radishes
1 cup (4 ounces)
   grated Cheddar
   cheese

Spread roll dough on baking sheet or jellyroll pan, lightly pressing seams and perforations to form solid layer of dough. Bake at 350° for 10 to 12 minutes. Let stand until cool. Combine cream cheese, mayonnaise and salad dressing mix, blending until smooth. Spread mixture on cooled crust. In layers, add broccoli, cauliflower, green pepper, tomatoes, radishes and cheese. Chill before serving. Yield: 16 to 24 servings.

Zucchini Appetizers

Combine zucchini, onion, baking mix and cheese, mixing thoroughly. Stir in parsley, salt, seasoned salt, oregano, black pepper and garlic. Add oil and eggs. Pour batter into greased 13x9x3-inch baking pan. Bake at 350° for about 25 minutes or until golden brown. Cut into bite-sized squares. Yield: 8 dozen.

3 cups thinly-sliced unpeeled zucchini
½ cup minced onion
1 cup biscuit baking mix
½ cup (2 ounces) grated Parmesan cheese
2 tablespoons chopped parsley
½ teaspoon salt
½ teaspoon seasoned salt
½ teaspoon dried oregano
Dash of black pepper
1 clove garlic, minced
½ cup vegetable oil
4 eggs, lightly beaten

Spiced Tea Mix

Combine tea, orange juice granules, sugar, cloves, cinnamon and allspice, mixing thoroughly. Store in tightly covered container. Combine 2 to 3 teaspoons of mixture with 1 cup hot water, stirring until sugar is dissolved. Yield: 5½ cups.

1 cup lemon-flavored instant tea powder
2 cups instant orange juice granules
3½ cups sugar
1 tablespoon ground cloves
1 tablespoon cinnamon
1 teaspoon allspice

Cheesy Artichoke Appetizers

2 8-ounce cans
   refrigerated
   crescent dinner
   rolls
¾ cup (3 ounces)
   shredded
   mozzarella cheese
1 3-ounce can grated
   Parmesan cheese
½ cup Miracle Whip
   salad dressing
1 14-ounce can
   artichoke hearts,
   drained and
   chopped
1 4-ounce can
   chopped green
   chilies, drained
   (optional)

Unroll dough into rectangles; press onto bottom and sides of 15x10x1-inch jelly roll pan to form crust. Bake at 375° for 10 mintues. Combine remaining ingredients; mix well. Spread over crust. Bake at 375° for 15 minutes or until cheese is melted. Let stand 5 minutes before serving.

Super Honey Slush

6 cups water
1½ cups honey
1 46-ounce can
   pineapple juice
3 6-ounce cans frozen
   lemonade
   concentrate,
   undiluted
5 bananas, mashed
   Lemon-lime
   carbonated soft
   drink

Combine water and honey, bring to a boil, remove from heat and let stand until cool. Stir in pineapple juice, lemonade and bananas. Pour juice mixture into 5-quart plastic ice cream bucket. Freeze, stirring after 2 to 3 hours, until firm. To serve, scoop portions into individual glasses and add soft drink, stirring to form slush. Yield: 8 quarts.

Banana Crush Punch

Dissolve sugar in water. Add pine-apple, lemon and orange juices and bananas, mixing thoroughly. Pour juice mixture into clean waxed milk cartons. Freeze until firm. To serve, place frozen juice block in punch bowl. Pour ginger ale over block. Punch will be slush consistency. Yield: 12 quarts.

Note: Juice mixture may be frozen in ring-shaped mold.

4 cups sugar
6 cups water
1 14-ounce can pineapple juice
1 12-ounce can frozen lemon concentrate, undiluted
2 12-ounce cans frozen orange juice concentrate, undiluted
6 bananas, mashed
7 28-ounce bottles ginger ale

Party Punch

Combine, orange juice, limeade, lemonade, pineapple juice, cranberry juice and water. Chill until ready to serve. Pour juice mixture into punch bowl. Add ginger ale and club soda. Yield: 7 quarts.

Note: Juice mixture may be frozen in ring-shaped mold with maraschino cherries and lemon or orange slices.

1 6-ounce can frozen orange juice concentrate, undiluted
2 6-ounce cans frozen limeade concentrate, undiluted
2 6-ounce cans frozen lemonade concentrate, undiluted
1 46-ounce can pineapple juice
2 cups cranberry juice
4 cups water
2 quarts ginger ale
2 cups club soda

Orange Honey Drink

1 cup milk
1 cup water
3½ tablespoons honey
¾ cup orange juice
1 teaspoon vanilla
10 ice cubes

Combine milk, water, honey, orange juice and vanilla in blender container. Add ice cubes. Blend until slush consistency. Yield: 4 to 5 cups.

Tomato Juice Cocktail

4 quarts tomato juice
1 cup sugar
3 tablespoons lemon juice
3 tablespoons salt
½ teaspoon black pepper
1 tablespoon celery seed
1 teaspoon hot pepper sauce

Combine tomato juice, sugar, lemon juice, salt, black pepper, celery seed and hot pepper sauce in stock pot. Bring to a boil and boil for 10 minutes. Pour into hot sterilized canning jars. Seal, according to manufacturer's directions, with hot lids and rings. Rings may be removed after 12 hours. Yield: 4 quarts.

Hot Mocha Mix

1 cup unsweetened cocoa
2 cups sugar
2 cups nonfat dry milk powder
2 cups nondairy coffee creamer powder
½ cup instant coffee granules
1 vanilla bean, quartered

Combine cocoa, sugar, milk and creamer powder, coffee granules and vanilla bean, blending thoroughly. Divide mixture into 4 jars, placing vanilla bean piece in each. Seal and store in refrigerator for at least 1 week before using. Combine 3 tablespoons with ¾ cup boiling water, stirring until sugar is dissolved. Add marshmallow or whipped cream, if desired. Yield: 7½ cups.

BREAKING BREAD

*T*hey broke bread
in their homes and
ate together with glad
and sincere hearts.
ACTS 2: 46-47

B   R   E   A   D   S

Great Buttermilk Biscuits

2½ **cups all-purpose flour**
4 **teaspoons baking powder**
1 **teaspoon baking soda**
½ **teaspoon salt**
2 **tablespoons vegetable oil**
1½ **cups buttermilk**
3 **tablespoons vegetable oil**

Combine flour, baking powder, baking soda and salt. Combine oil and buttermilk. Add to dry ingredients, stirring to combine. More flour or buttermilk may be added to form dough with slightly sticky consistency. Knead on lightly-floured surface 5 or 6 times. Press dough to ¾-inch thickness and cut with 3-inch biscuit cutter. Spread oil on pizza baking pan. Place biscuits on oil, turning once. Bake at 350° for 15 to 20 minutes or until golden brown. Yield: 20.

Sweet Potato Drop Biscuits

3 **cups all-purpose flour**
¼ **cup firmly-packed brown sugar**
1 **tablespoon baking soda**
½ **teaspoon baking powder**
1½ **teaspoons salt**
⅓ **cup butter flavored vegetable shortening**
1 **16-ounce can sweet potatoes, drained and cubed**
1⅓ **cups buttermilk**

Combine flour, brown sugar, baking soda, baking powder and salt. Using pastry blender or 2 knives, cut shortening into dry ingredients until consistency of coarse crumbs. Add sweet potatoes and buttermilk, stirring just until ingredients are blended. Drop dough by heaping tablespoons about 1 inch apart on baking sheets. Bake at 450° for about 15 minutes or until golden brown. Serve warm or cool. To reheat, wrap biscuits in aluminum foil and bake in preheated oven at 450° for 10 minutes. Yield: 15.

Yeast Biscuits

Dissolve yeast in warm water. Sift flour, baking powder, baking soda, salt and sugar together. Using pastry blender or 2 knives, cut shortening into dry ingredients until size of peas. Stir in dissolved yeast and buttermilk. Roll dough to ½-inch thickness, cut with biscuit cutter and place on baking sheet. Bake at 400° for 20 to 25 minutes. Yield: 2½ dozen.

Note: Dough may be stored in refrigerator for a few days.

1 envelope dry yeast
¼ cup warm (110° to 115°) water
5 cups all-purpose flour
1 tablespoon baking powder
1 teaspoon baking soda
1 teaspoon salt
2 tablespoons sugar
1 cup vegetable shortening
2 cups buttermilk

Best Cornbread

Combine half and half and butter in saucepan. Heat to scald milk. Combine biscuit mix, cornmeal, sugar, baking soda and salt. Add milk mixture to dry ingredients, stirring lightly but thoroughly. Stir in eggs. Pour batter into greased and floured 13x9x2-inch baking pan. Bake at 350° for 30 minutes. Let stand for a few minutes before cutting. Yield: 16 to 20 servings.

1 cup half and half
1 cup butter
2 cups biscuit baking mix
1 cup yellow cornmeal
¾ cup sugar
½ teaspoon baking soda
½ teaspoon salt
2 eggs, lightly beaten

Broccoli Cornbread

1 cup butter
2 8½-ounce packages
  cornbread mix
1 small onion,
  chopped
1 10-ounce package
  frozen chopped
  broccoli, thawed
  and drained
1 cup small curd
  cottage cheese
4 eggs

Place butter in 13x9x2-inch baking dish. Bake at 350° until butter is melted. Combine cornbread mix, onion, broccoli, cottage cheese and eggs, mixing thoroughly. Stir in melted butter. Pour batter into baking dish. Bake at 350° for 45 minutes. Yield: 16 to 20 servings.

Mexican Cornbread

2 eggs, lightly beaten
1 cup sour cream
⅔ cup vegetable oil
1 16-ounce can cream
  style corn
1½ cups self-rising
  cornmeal
1 teaspoon salt
2 tablespoons
  chopped green bell
  pepper
1½ jalapeño peppers,
  chopped
1 cup (4 ounces)
  grated Cheddar
  cheese

Combine eggs, sour cream, oil and corn. Add cornmeal, salt, green pepper, jalapeño pepper and cheese. Pour batter into 8x8x2-inch baking pan. Bake at 350° for about 20 minutes. Yield: 9 servings.

Banana Nut Muffins

Sift flour, baking soda and salt to-gether. Add sugar, eggs, oil and buttermilk to dry ingredients, stirring until blended. Fold in bananas and pecans. Spoon batter into paper-lined muffin pans. Bake at 325° for 30 to 35 minutes. Yield: 1 dozen.

- 1½ cups all-purpose flour
- ¾ teaspoon baking soda
- ½ teaspoon salt
- 1 cup sugar
- 2 eggs
- ¾ cup vegetable oil
- 3 tablespoons buttermilk
- 1 cup mashed bananas
- ½ cup chopped pecans

Bran Muffins

Combine 1 cup cereal, boiling water and oil, mixing thoroughly. Combine flour, sugar, baking soda, salt and 2 cups cereal. Add eggs and buttermilk to dry ingredients, blending well. Stir in soaked cereal mixture. Add raisins and pecans. Spoon batter into muffin pans prepared with non-stick vegetable spray. Bake at 400° for 15 to 20 minutes. Yield: 2½ dozen.

Note: Batter may be stored, covered, in refrigerator for up to 6 weeks.

- 3 cups bran cereal, divided
- 1 cup boiling water
- ½ cup vegetable oil
- 2½ cups all-purpose flour
- 1½ cups sugar
- 2½ teaspoons baking soda
- 1 teaspoon salt
- 2 eggs, beaten
- 2 cups buttermilk
- 1 cup seedless raisins (optional)
- 1 cup finely chopped pecans

Garden Spice Muffins

- ½ **cup finely shredded carrots**
- ½ **cup finely shredded zucchini**
- 3½ **cups oat bran cereal**
- 1½ **cups skim milk**
- 2 **egg whites**
- 2 **tablespoons vegetable oil**
- ½ **teaspoon vanilla**
- 1½ **cups all-purpose flour**
- ⅓ **cup firmly-packed brown sugar**
- 1 **tablespoon baking powder**
- 1½ **teaspoons cinnamon**
- ¼ **teaspoon ground cloves**

Combine carrots, zucchini, bran cereal, milk, egg whites, oil and vanilla, mixing thoroughly. Let stand for 5 minutes. Combine flour, sugar, baking powder, cinnamon and cloves in large mixing bowl. Add liquid mixture to dry ingredients, stirring just until moistened. Spoon batter into paper-lined muffin pans. Bake at 400° for 20 to 25 minutes. Yield: 1 dozen.

Banana Bran Bread

- 1 **cup all-purpose flour**
- 1 **cup bran (not cereal)**
- ½ **cup powdered milk**
- ⅔ **cup firmly-packed brown sugar**
- 1 **tablespoon baking powder**
- 3 or 4 **small very ripe bananas, mashed**
- ½ **cup vegetable oil**
- 2 **eggs**
- ½ **cup chopped pecans**

Combine flour, bran, powdered milk, brown sugar and baking powder. Combine bananas, oil and eggs. Gradually add dry ingredients to banana mixture, mixing thoroughly. Stir in pecans. Pour batter into greased 9x5x3-inch loaf pan. Bake at 350° for 50 to 60 minutes or until center is firm. Cool in pan for 10 minutes, then invert on wire rack. Yield: 1 loaf.

Banana Nut Bread

Combine flour, sugar and salt. Stir in oil, eggs and vanilla. Dissolve baking soda in sour milk and add to egg mixture. Stir in bananas and pecans. Pour batter into 2 greased and floured 9x5x3-inch loaf pans or ring molds. Bake at 350° for 1 hour or until wooden pick inserted near center comes out clean; do not overbake. Yield: 2 loaves.

> 2¼ **cups all-purpose flour**
> 2 **cups sugar**
> ½ **teaspoon salt**
> ¾ **cup vegetable oil or melted shortening, cooled**
> 3 **eggs**
> 1 **teaspoon vanilla**
> ⅓ **teaspoon baking soda**
> ¼ **cup sour milk**
> 4 **large bananas, mashed**
> 1 **cup chopped pecans (optional)**

Lemon Bread

Cream shortening and sugar together until smooth. Combine eggs and milk. Add to creamed mixture. Sift flour, baking powder and salt together. Add dry ingredients to liquid mixture, mixing thoroughly. Add lemon peel. Pour batter into 2 greased and floured 9x5x3-inch loaf pans. Bake at 300° for 1 hour and 15 minutes. Pour lemon topping over hot loaves. Yield: 2 loaves

> 1 **cup shortening or margarine, softened**
> 2 **cups sugar**
> 2 **eggs, beaten**
> 1 **cup milk**
> 3 **cups all-purpose flour**
> 2 **teaspoons baking powder**
> 1 **teaspoon salt**
> 1 **lemon peel, grated**

Topping
> **Juice of 3 lemons**
> 1½ **cups sugar**

Combine lemon juice and sugar, blending thoroughly. Pour topping over hot loaves.

Pear Bread

½ **cup butter, softened**
1 **cup sugar**
2 **eggs**
2 **cups all-purpose flour**
1 **teaspoon baking powder**
½ **teaspoon baking soda**
½ **teaspoon salt**
¼ **cup yogurt or buttermilk**
1 **cup coarsely chopped or mashed peeled pears**
1 **teaspoon vanilla**
½ **cup chopped nuts (optional)**

Cream butter, sugar and eggs together until smooth. Combine flour, baking powder, baking soda and salt. Add dry ingredients and yogurt to creamed mixture. Stir in pears, vanilla and nuts. Pour batter into greased 9x5x3-inch loaf pan. Bake at 350° for 1 hour. Yield: 1 loaf.

Pineapple Squash Bread

3 **cups all-purpose flour**
2 **teaspoons baking soda**
½ **teaspoon baking powder**
1 **teaspoon salt**
3 **eggs, lightly beaten**
2 **cups sugar**
1 **cup vegetable oil**
2 **teaspoons vanilla**
2 **cups chopped yellow squash or zucchini**
1 **8-ounce can crushed pineapple, well drained**

Sift flour, baking soda, baking powder and salt together. Combine eggs, sugar, oil and vanilla, beating until creamy. Add squash and pineapple to creamed mixture. Stir in dry ingredients. Spread batter in 2 well-greased and floured 8x4x3-inch loaf pans. Bake at 350° for 1 hour or until wooden pick inserted near center comes out clean. Cool in pan for 10 minutes, then invert on wire rack. Yield: 2 loaves.

Pumpkin Bread

Combine eggs, sugar and oil. Add pumpkin, beating until smooth. Sift flour, baking powder, baking soda, salt, allspice, cinnamon, cloves and nutmeg together. Add dry ingredients to pumpkin mixture. Stir in nuts and water. Pour batter into 2 greased and floured 9x5x3-inch loaf pans. Bake at 350° for 1 hour or until wooden pick inserted near center comes out clean.

4 eggs, beaten
3 cups sugar
1 cup vegetable oil
1 16-ounce can pumpkin
3½ cups all-purpose flour
1 teaspoon baking powder
1 teaspoon baking soda
½ teaspoon salt
1 teaspoon allspice
1 teaspoon cinnamon
1 teaspoon ground cloves
1 teaspoon nutmeg
¾ cup chopped nuts
⅔ cup water

Oatmeal Bread

Combine oats, honey and 1 cup warm water. Let stand for 2 hours. Dissolve yeast and sugar in 1½ cups warm water. Stir in powdered milk. Combine oat mixture, yeast mixture and salt, stirring well. Add flour and mix to form dough. Knead by hand. Place dough in ungreased bowl, cover and let rise until doubled in bulk. Punch down and let rise again. Punch down and shape into two loaves. Place in oiled 9x5x3-inch loaf pans, turning dough once to coat top with oil. Let rise, covered, until doubled in bulk. Bake at 450° for 25 to 30 minutes. Yield: 2 loaves.

1½ cups uncooked rolled oats
¼ cup honey
1 cup warm water
2 envelopes dry yeast
1½ tablespoons sugar
1½ cups warm (110° to 115°) water
½ cup skim powdered milk
1 tablespoon salt
5 to 5½ cups unsifted all-purpose flour

Grandmother's Gingerbread

½ cup butter or margarine, softened
½ cup sugar
1 egg, beaten
1 cup molasses
2½ cups sifted all-purpose flour
1½ teaspoons baking soda
½ teaspoon salt
1 teaspoon cinnamon
1 teaspoon ginger
1 teaspoon ground cloves
1 cup hot water

Cream butter and sugar together until smooth. Add egg and molasses. Sift flour, baking soda, salt, cinnamon, ginger and ground cloves together twice. Add dry ingredients to molasses mixture, mixing thoroughly. Add hot water and beat until smooth. Pour batter into 12x8x2-inch baking pan. Bake at 350° for 25 to 30 minutes, remove from oven and sprinkle with topping. Continue baking for 10 minutes. Serve with whipped cream. Yield: 12 to 16 servings

Topping

⅓ cup butter or margarine, melted
½ cup firmly-packed brown sugar
¼ cup all-purpose flour
1 teaspoon cinnamon
½ teaspoon grated lemon peel
½ cup chopped walnuts or pecans

Combine butter, brown sugar, flour, cinnamon, lemon peel and nuts. Sprinkle over partially baked gingerbread.

SEASON
WITH SALT

*L*et your conversation
be always full of grace,
seasoned with salt,
so that you may know
how to answer everyone.

COLOSSIANS 4. 6

SOUPS & SALADS

Beef Vegetable Soup

1½ pounds beef stew
    meat
    Water
½ cup barley
1 16-ounce can
    tomatoes
1 large onion,
    chopped
½ green bell pepper,
    chopped
3 stalks celery,
    chopped
4 small potatoes,
    cubed
4 carrots, diced
1 cup shredded
    cabbage
1 cup chopped okra
½ jalapeño pepper,
    diced (optional)
    Parsley to taste
3 beef bouillon cubes
    Salt and black
    pepper to taste

Place beef in stockpot and add water to measure 1 inch above beef. Add barley and cook for 30 minutes. Add tomatoes, onion, green pepper, celery, potatoes, carrots, cabbage, okra, jalapeño pepper, parsley and bouillon. Simmer until vegetables and beef are tender. Season with salt and black pepper. Yield: 8 to 10 servings.

Quick Chili

Sauté onion, garlic and green pepper in bacon drippings in stockpot for 10 minutes, stirring occasionally. Add beef and sauté for 1 minute. Combine chili powder, water and tomatoes in saucepan. Add bay leaf, salt, cumin and cayenne pepper. Bring to a boil. Add beans to beef, then add tomato mixture. Simmer, covered, for 30 minutes to 1 hour. Yield: 6 to 8 servings.

1 large onion, chopped
1 clove garlic, crushed
1 green bell pepper, shredded lengthwise
2 tablespoons bacon drippings or butter
1 pound lean ground beef
1 16-ounce can kidney beans, drained
2½ tablespoons chili powder
¼ cup cold water
1 cup canned tomatoes with juice
1 bay leaf
1½ teaspoons salt
½ teaspoon cumin seed or ¼ teaspoon ground cumin
Dash of cayenne pepper

Taco Soup

1 pound ground beef
½ medium-sized
   onion, chopped
2 cloves garlic,
   minced
½ 16-ounce can corn
1 16-ounce can
   kidney beans or
   chili without beans
1 4-ounce can black
   olives, drained and
   sliced
1 13-ounce can
   tomatoes with green
   chilies
1 cup tomato juice
1 teaspoon salt
   (optional)
½ teaspoon black
   pepper
½ teaspoon chili
   powder
½ teaspoon cumin
1 10¾-ounce can
   cream of Cheddar
   cheese soup, diluted
   with water

Sauté beef, onion and garlic together in stockpot until beef is browned. Drain excess fat. Add corn, beans, olives, tomatoes, tomato juice, salt, black pepper, chili powder, cumin and diluted soup. Simmer for about 30 minutes. Check seasoning, adjusting to taste. Yield: 8 to 10 servings.

Hamburger Soup

Combine bouillon, water and tomatoes in stockpot. Bring to a boil. Add mixed vegetables, corn and bay leaves. Stir in ground beef and noodles. Simmer until flavors are well blended and noodles are tender. Yield: 10 to 12 servings.

6 beef bouillon cubes

4 cups water

1 28-ounce can tomatoes, crushed

2 10-ounce packages frozen mixed vegetables

1 16-ounce can corn

2 bay leaves

1½ to 2 pounds ground beef, browned, drained and crumbled

1 to 1½ cups medium egg noodles (optional)

Broccoli Soup

Pour broth into stockpot and heat until steaming. Add cheese to broth, stirring to melt. Add white sauce, broccoli and tomatoes. Season with garlic, parsley and cayenne pepper. Simmer until thoroughly hot and slightly thickened. Yield: 12 servings.

3 quarts low-sodium chicken broth

4 cups (16 ounces) cubed pasteurized process cheese spread

2 cups white sauce

1 10-ounce package frozen chopped broccoli, thawed and drained

1 13-ounce can tomatoes with green chilies

Garlic powder

Parsley flakes

Cayenne pepper (optional)

Cabbage Soup

1 **head cabbage,
    shredded**
1 **cup sliced carrot**
¾ **cup sliced onions**
1 **small turnip, diced**
½ **cup sliced celery**
1 **cup cubed potatoes**
1 **tablespoon
    vegetable oil**
1 **tablespoon butter**
4 **cups water**
2 **cups chicken broth**
¼ **teaspoon black
    pepper**
¼ **teaspoon thyme**

Cook cabbage, carrot, onions, turnip, celery and potatoes in oil and butter in 4-quart saucepan over medium heat for 4 to 5 minutes or until cabbage is soft. Add water, broth, black pepper and thyme. Bring to a boil, then simmer for 30 minutes. Yield: 8 to 10 servings.

Cactus Soup

3 **cups cubed fresh
    cactus or canned
    cactus**
1 **large onion,
    chopped**
4 **cups canned
    tomatoes with juice,
    chopped**
½ to 1 **pound ground
    beef, cooked,
    drained and
    crumbled**
3 to 5 **potatoes, diced
    Chili powder to
    taste
    Salt and black
    pepper to taste**

Combine cactus, onion, tomatoes and beef in stockpot. Simmer for 10 minutes. Add potatoes and cook until tender. Season with chili powder, salt and black pepper. Yield: 8 servings.

Cheese Soup

Sauté onion, celery and carrots in butter in stockpot until tender. Add broth. Simmer, covered, for 20 minutes. Stir in potato soup and cheese. Season with parsley, hot pepper sauce, salt and black pepper. Add sour cream. Simmer for 15 minutes. Stir in sherry. Yield: 8 servings.

3 **green onions, chopped**
3 **stalks celery with leaves, chopped**
2 **carrots, grated**
¼ **cup butter or margarine**
2 **10¾-ounce cans chicken broth**
2 **10¾-ounce cans potato soup, undiluted**
2 **cups (8 ounces) grated Cheddar or American cheese**
  Parsley flakes
  Few drops of hot pepper sauce
  Salt and coarsely ground black pepper to taste
1 **cup sour cream**
3 **tablespoons sherry**

Nancy's Chicken Soup

3 pounds chicken, cut
  up
  Water
1 whole yellow onion
  Stalks of celery
  without leaves
1 sprig parsley
1 tablespoon dill
  weed
3 to 4 tablespoons
  chicken bouillon
  granules
  White pepper to
  taste
2 large carrots, sliced
  and cooked

Remove excess fat and fatted skin from chicken. Place in 5-quart stockpot and add cold water to fill ¾ full. Bring to a boil. Skim froth from surface. Add onion, celery, parsley, dill weed and bouillon. Simmer for 2 to 3 hours or until chicken is tender. Remove chicken from broth, discard bones and skin and cut into bite-sized pieces. Return chicken to broth, season with white pepper and add cooked carrots. Yield: 8 servings.

Rich Onion Soup

6 onions, sliced
6 tablespoons butter
2 tablespoons corn oil
½ teaspoon sugar
½ teaspoon dry
  mustard
3 tablespoons all-
  purpose flour
2 quarts beef broth
1½ cups white cooking
  wine (optional)
  Salt and black
  pepper to taste
  French bread slices
  Gruyère cheese
  slices
  Grated Parmesan
  cheese (optional)

Cook onions in butter and oil in stockpot over low heat for 30 minutes, stirring occasionally. Add sugar and mustard. Simmer for 30 minutes. Blend in flour, then stir in broth and wine. Simmer for 30 minutes. Season with salt and black pepper to taste. Ladle soup into individual oven-proof soup crocks. Cover each serving with bread and Gruyère cheese slice. Bake in preheated oven at 400° or under broiler until cheese is bubbly. Sprinkle with Parmesan cheese. Yield: 8 servings.

Zesty Cheese Potato Soup

Combine broth, bouillon, chicken, onion, potatoes and carrots in stockpot. Cook until vegetables are tender. Stir in peas, milk and cheeses. Cook until thickened. Yield: 12 to 15 servings.

4 cups chicken broth
2 chicken bouillon cubes
3 cups diced cooked chicken
1 tablespoon onion flakes
3 cups diced potatoes
4 carrots, sliced
1 16-ounce can peas
½ cup milk
1 12-ounce jar pasteurized process cheese spread
1 cup (4 ounces) cubed pasteurized process cheese spread

Potato Soup

Sauté onion in margarine until tender. Add onion to potatoes in stockpot. Stir in soups, season with salt and black pepper and add milk to preferred consistency. Simmer until flavors are blended. Yield: 8 to 12 servings.

Variation: Sauté 6 slices turkey bacon, remove from skillet, drain and crumble. Sauté onion in margarine added to bacon drippings. Sprinkle bacon bits on individual servings of soup. Cream of broccoli soup may be substituted for other cream soups.

1 large onion, chopped
½ cup margarine
8 cups diced potatoes, cooked and drained
1 10¾-ounce can cream of mushroom soup, undiluted
1 10¾-ounce can cream of chicken soup, undiluted
Salt and black pepper to taste
Milk

Pennsylvania Dutch Salmon Soup

2 potatoes, diced
2 stalks celery,
  chopped
1 carrot, grated
6 scallions with green
  tips, chopped
  Water
1 16-ounce can cream
  style corn
  Salt and black
  pepper to taste
1 15-ounce can
  salmon, drained
  and liquid reserved

Combine potatoes, celery, carrot and scallions in large saucepan. Add water to measure 3 inches above vegetables. Cook for 10 minutes. Stir in corn, salt and black pepper. Remove bone and skin from salmon. Flake salmon and add with reserved liquid to vegetables. Simmer until thoroughly heated. Yield: 8 servings.

Note: *Soup be may frozen.*

Mayberry's Salad

Salad
1 head lettuce,
  chopped
1 head cauliflower,
  chopped
1 pound bacon,
  cooked, drained
  and crumbled

Combine lettuce, cauliflower and bacon bits. Add dressing, mixing lightly but thoroughly. Yield: 8 to 10 servings.

Dressing
1 cup mayonnaise
  (not low-fat)
¾ cup sugar
¾ cup (3 ounces)
  shredded fresh
  Parmesan cheese

Combine mayonnaise, sugar and cheese. Add dressing to vegetable mixture.

Three Bean Salad

Salad

>1 16-ounce can yellow
>   wax beans, drained
>1 16-ounce can red
>   beans or kidney
>   beans, drained
>1 16-ounce can cut
>   green beans,
>   drained
>¼ to ½ cup thinly sliced
>   carrots
>1 stalk celery, thinly
>   sliced

Dressing

>½ cup vinegar
>½ cup vegetable oil
>½ cup sugar
>1 tablespoon salt

Combine beans, carrots and celery in heat-proof bowl. Pour hot dressing over bean mixture. Chill overnight. Yield: 8 to 10 servings.

Combine vinegar, oil, sugar and salt in saucepan. Bring to a boil and cook until sugar and salt are dissolved. Pour hot dressing over bean mixture.

Faye's Broccoli Salad

Salad

>½ pound bacon,
>   cooked, drained
>   and crumbled
>1 cup chopped red
>   onion
>1 cup raisins
>2 bunches broccoli,
>   flowerets only

Dressing

>2 cups mayonnaise
>¼ cup vinegar
>½ cup sugar

Combine bacon, onion, raisins and broccoli. Stir in dressing, mixing lightly but thoroughly. Chill for at least 3 hours. Yield: 8 to 10 servings.

Combine mayonnaise, vinegar and sugar, mixing until smooth. Add to broccoli mixture.

Green Bean Salad with Bacon

Salad

    1 **pound fresh green beans, cut in 1-inch pieces**
    Boiling water
    4 **slices bacon, cooked, drained and crumbled**
    1 **small red onion, thinly sliced**

Cook beans in 1-inch boiling water for about 7 minutes or until crisp tender; do not salt. Drain and set aside to cool. Combine beans with bacon and onion, reserving a few bacon bits and onion rings for garnish. Pour dressing over bean mixture, tossing to thoroughly coat beans. Chill for 1 hour, tossing again just before serving. Garnish with onion and bacon. Yield: 4 servings.

Dressing

    3 **tablespoons cider vinegar**
    2 **tablespoons vegetable oil**
    1 **teaspoon sugar**
    1 **teaspoon salt**
    ¼ **teaspoon black pepper**
    ⅛ **teaspoon dried thyme**

Combine vinegar, oil, sugar, salt, black pepper and thyme in container with tightly-fitting lid. Shake until sugar and salt are dissolved. Pour dressing over bean mixture.

German Potato Salad

    6 **slices bacon**
    6 **medium-sized white potatoes, cooked and sliced**
    ¼ **cup minced onion**
    ½ **cup vinegar**
    ¼ **cup sugar**
    1 **teaspoon salt**
    Black pepper to taste

Sauté bacon until crisp, remove from skillet, drain and crumble. Add bacon to potatoes. Sauté onion in bacon drippings until partially tender. Add vinegar and sugar to onion. Bring to a boil. Pour pan liquids over potato mixture. Season with salt and black pepper. Mix lightly but thoroughly. Yield: 6 servings.

Cabbage Slaw

Slaw

Combine cabbage, green pepper, celery, carrots, onion and celery seed. Add dressing to cabbage mixture, mixing lightly but thoroughly. Chill until ready to serve. Yield: 12 to 16 servings.

- **1 head cabbage, shredded**
- **1 cup chopped green bell pepper**
- **2 cups diced celery**
- **1 cup shredded carrots**
- **½ cup chopped green onion**
- **2 teaspoons celery seed**

Dressing

Combine mayonnaise, vinegar, sugar, salt, celery seed and mustard, blending until smooth. Add dressing to cabbage mixture.

- **4 cups mayonnaise**
- **1 cup cider vinegar**
- **1½ cups sugar**
- **2 tablespoons salt**
- **3 tablespoons celery seed**
- **2 tablespoons prepared mustard**

Super Coleslaw

Slaw

1 3-pound head
  cabbage, finely
  shredded
1 medium-sized
  onion, chopped
1 medium-sized green
  bell pepper,
  chopped
½ cup chopped celery
¼ teaspoon black
  pepper

Combine cabbage, onion, green pepper, celery and black pepper in container with tightly-fitting lid. Pour dressing over vegetable mixture. Chill, covered, overnight. Yield: 6 to 8 servings.

Dressing

1 cup white vinegar
1 cup vegetable oil
1 cup sugar
1 tablespoon salt
¼ teaspoon black
  pepper
½ teaspoon dry
  mustard

Combine vinegar, oil, sugar, salt, black pepper and mustard in saucepan. Bring to a boil. Pour dressing over cabbage mixture.

Fruited Carrot Salad

2 cups shredded
  carrots
1 8-ounce can
  pineapple tidbits,
  undrained
½ cup chopped apple
¼ cup raisins
½ cup orange juice

Combine carrots, pineapple, apple, raisins and orange juice, tossing lightly to mix. Chill, covered, until ready to serve.

Copper Pennies

Combine warm carrots, onion and green pepper in salad bowl. Pour dressing over carrot mixture. Let cool to room temperature, then chill overnight. Serve hot or cold.

Combine soup, sugar, oil, vinegar, Worcestershire sauce, mustard, salt and black pepper, mixing thoroughly. Pour dressing over carrot mixture, mixing well.

Salad

    2 pounds carrots, sliced, cooked and drained
    1 medium-sized onion, chopped or sliced
    1 green bell pepper, chopped or sliced

Dressing

    1 10½-ounce can tomato soup, undiluted
    ¾ to 1 cup sugar
    ½ cup salad oil
    ½ to ¾ cup vinegar
    1 teaspoon Worcestershire sauce
    1 teaspoon mustard
    Salt and black pepper to taste

Pea Salad

Rinse peas in running hot water to thaw, then drain. Combine peas, bacon, cauliflower, onion, celery and cheese. Add mayonnaise to taste. Chill. Yield: 8 to 10 servings.

    1 16-ounce package frozen peas
    1 16-ounce package bacon, cooked, drained and diced
    1 cup chopped cauliflower
    ½ cup chopped onion
    ½ cup chopped celery
    1 cup (4 ounces) grated cheese
    Mayonnaise

Mandarin Spinach Salad

1½ **pounds fresh spinach**
6 **slices bacon**
3 **hard-cooked eggs, chopped**
2 **11-ounce cans mandarin oranges, drained**
½ **cup vegetable oil**
¼ **cup ketchup**
2 **tablespoons vinegar**
1 **tablespoon Worcestershire sauce**
⅓ **cup sugar**
Salt to taste
¼ **onion, grated**

Rinse, drain and blot spinach with paper towel. Cut away stems and tear leaves into bite-sized pieces. Sauté bacon until crisp. Remove from skillet, reserving 1 tablespoon drippings. Crumble bacon. Combine spinach, bacon bits, eggs and oranges. Blend oil, ketchup, vinegar, Worcestershire sauce, sugar, salt and onion with bacon drippings, stirring until sugar is dissolved. Pour dressing over spinach mixture. Yield: 6 servings.

Zucchini Salad

Salad
   3 **medium zucchini, thinly sliced**
   ½ **cup chopped green bell pepper**
   ½ **cup chopped celery**
   ½ **cup chopped onion**

Dressing
   ⅔ **cup fresh lemon juice**
   ¼ **cup red cooking wine**
   2 **tablespoons red wine vinegar**
   ⅓ **cup vegetable oil**
   ½ **cup sugar**
   1 **teaspoon salt**
   ⅛ **teaspoon black pepper**

Combine zucchini, green pepper, celery and onion. Pour dressing over zucchini mixture, mixing lightly but thoroughly. Chill, covered, for at least 6 hours. Salad may be stored in refrigerator for up to 2 weeks. Yield: 6 to 8 servings.

Combine lemon juice, wine, wine vinegar, oil, sugar, salt and black pepper in container with tightly-fitting lid. Shake until sugar and salt are dissolved. Pour dressing over zucchini mixture.

Gazpacho Salad

Salad

1 **large cucumber,
   thinly sliced**
2 **medium tomatoes,
   chopped**
1 **large carrot, thinly
   sliced**
1 **small red onion,
   thinly sliced**
1 **large stalk celery,
   thinly sliced**

*Combine cucumber, tomatoes, carrot,
onion and celery. Pour dressing over
vegetable mixture, tossing lightly but
gently. Chill, covered, overnight. Stir
several times. Yield: 6 to 8 servings.*

Dressing

⅓ **cup vegetable oil**
2 **tablespoons red
   wine vinegar**
2 **tablespoons
   vegetable or tomato
   juice**
1 **teaspoon sugar
   Salt and freshly
   ground black
   pepper**

*Combine oil, vinegar, juice, sugar, salt
and black pepper in container with
tightly-fitting lid. Shake until sugar
and salt are dissolved. Pour dressing
over vegetable mixture.*

Sweet-Sour Vegetable Salad

Salad
- 1 16-ounce can whole kernel corn, drained
- 1 16-ounce can cut green beans, drained
- 2 cups frozen peas, thawed
- ½ cup chopped green bell pepper
- 1 cup sliced onion
- 1 cup chopped celery

Combine corn, green beans, peas, green pepper, onion and celery in heat-proof bowl. Pour dressing over vegetable mixture. Chill before serving. Yield: 10 to 12 servings.

Dressing
- ⅓ cup oil
- ¾ cup vinegar
- ¾ cup sugar
- 1 teaspoon salt
- ¼ teaspoon black pepper

Combine oil, vinegar, sugar, salt and black pepper in saucepan. Bring to a boil. Pour hot dressing over vegetables.

Marinated Salad

Salad

1 16-ounce can
  English peas,
  drained
1 16-ounce jar salad
  olives, drained and
  chopped
6 green onions with
  tops, sliced
2 cloves garlic, thinly
  sliced
1 cup French-cut
  green beans
1 cup chopped celery
1 cup thinly-sliced
  carrots
1 2-ounce package
  slivered almonds

Combine peas, olives, onion, garlic, green beans, celery, carrots and almonds in salad bowl. Pour dressing over vegetables, stirring thoroughly. Chill before serving. Yield: 8 to 10 servings.

Dressing

1 teaspoon paprika
1 teaspoon dry
  mustard
½ cup sugar
¼ cup vinegar
  Juice of 1 orange
  Juice of 1 lemon
1 teaspoon
  Worcestershire
  sauce

Combine paprika, mustard, sugar, vinegar, orange juice, lemon juice and Worcestershire sauce in container with tightly-fitting lid. Shake until sugar is dissolved. Pour dressing over vegetables.

Macaroni Salad

Combine water, salt, bay leaves, celery seed, garlic powder and seasoning salt in large saucepan. Bring to a boil. Add macaroni and cook until tender. Drain and rinse. Remove bay leaves. Combine macaroni, onion, celery, egg and olives. Stir in salad dressings, mixing lightly but thoroughly. Add cheese and ham, if desired. Yield: 8 servings.

- 3 quarts water
- 1 teaspoon salt
- 2 bay leaves
- 1 teaspoon celery seed
- ½ teaspoon garlic powder
- ½ teaspoon seasoning salt
- 1 16-ounce package elbow macaroni
- ½ cup chopped onion
- ½ cup chopped celery
- 3 hard-cooked eggs, chopped
- ¼ cup sliced black and green olives
- ½ cup mayonnaise-type salad dressing
- ¼ cup cucumber salad dressing
- Diced cheese (optional)
- Diced ham (optional)

Spaghetti Salad

1 **16-ounce package spaghetti, cooked and drained**
1 **large green bell pepper, chopped**
1 **large red onion, chopped**
2 **large tomatoes, chopped**
1 **8-ounce bottle Italian salad dressing**
⅓ **cup salad seasoning**

Combine spaghetti, green pepper, onion and tomatoes. Pour dressing over spaghetti mixture, sprinkle with salad seasoning and mix lightly but thoroughly. Yield: 10 to 12 servings.

Tortellini Salad

Salad
3 **cups cooked cheese-filled tortellini**
2 **cups broccoli flowerets, cooked**
1½ **cups sliced mushrooms**
1½ **cups cherry tomato halves**
1 **cup chopped zesty dill pickle**

Combine tortellini, broccoli, mushrooms, tomatoes and pickle. Pour dressing over tortellini mixture, mixing lightly but thoroughly. Chill, covered, for at least 4 hours. Yield: 8 to 10 servings.

Dressing
⅓ **cup vegetable oil**
2 **tablespoons wine vinegar**
2 **teaspoons Dijon mustard**
½ **teaspoon basil leaves**

Combine oil, vinegar, mustard and basil in container with tightly-fitting lid. Shake to blend liquids. Pour dressing over tortellini mixture.

Rice Salad

½ **cup Italian salad**
   dressing
1½ **cups water**
1 **cup uncooked**
   regular rice
1 **10-ounce package**
   frozen peas
1 **4-ounce can**
   chopped
   mushrooms,
   drained
1 **small cucumber,**
   chopped
3 **tablespoons minced**
   green onion
1 **8-ounce can water**
   chestnuts, drained
   and chopped
1 **2-ounce jar stuffed**
   olives, drained and
   chopped
½ **cup mayonnaise**

Combine salad dressing and water in saucepan. Bring to a boil. Add rice to liquid and cook over low heat for 25 minutes. Let stand until cool. Prepare peas according to package directions, cooking for 2 to 3 minutes. Drain well. Combine rice, peas, mushrooms, cucumber, onion, water chestnuts and olives. Add mayonnaise, mixing lightly but thoroughly. Chill for at least 1 hour. Salad may be prepared a day in advance and stored in refrigerator. Yield: 8 to 10 servings.

Tabbouleh

Salad

  1 cup fine or medium
    bulgar
    Water
  3 medium tomatoes,
    finely chopped
  1 cup chopped
    scallions
  3 cups finely chopped
    parsley
  1 cup finely chopped
    cucumbers
  ½ cup finely chopped
    fresh mint leaves

Soak bulgar in water to cover for 15 to 20 minutes or until tender. Drain thoroughly, pressing to remove excess water. Fluff to separate grains. Combine tomatoes, scallions, parsley, cucumbers and mint in salad bowl. Add bulgar and toss gently. Pour dressing over bulgar mixture, tossing gently to coat well. Chill, covered, until ready to serve. Spoon salad into lettuce-lined salad bowl. Serve with pita bread. Yield: 6 to 8 servings.

Dressing

  ½ cup olive oil
  ¼ to ⅓ cup fresh
    lemon juice
    Salt and freshly
    ground black
    pepper to taste

Combine oil, lemon juice, salt and black pepper in container with tightly-fitting lid. Shake well. Pour dressing over bulgar mixture.

Curried Chicken Salad

Salad
  3 **cups diced cooked chicken**
  1 **20-ounce can pineapple chunks, drained**
  ½ **cup slivered almonds**
  ⅓ **cup golden raisins**
  1 **red apple, diced**
  2 **tablespoons shredded coconut**

Dressing
  3 **tablespoons minced green onion**
  2 **tablespoons butter**
  1¼ **teaspoons curry powder**
  ⅓ **cup mayonnaise**
  1 **tablespoon lemon juice**
  ½ **teaspoon salt**
    Dash of cayenne pepper

Combine chicken, pineapple, almonds, raisins and apple. Add dressing, tossing gently to mix. Pour chicken mixture into lettuce-lined salad bowl and sprinkle with coconut. Yield: 4 to 6 servings.

Sauté onion in butter with curry powder for 3 to 4 minutes. Let stand until cool. Combine onion mixture with mayonnaise, lemon juice, salt and cayenne pepper, blending thoroughly. Add to chicken mixture.

Baked Hot Chicken Salad

4 cups diced cooked
   chicken
⅓ cup sliced
   mushrooms
2 cups diced celery
½ cup chopped onion
½ cup diced green bell
   pepper
½ cup slivered
   almonds, toasted
½ teaspoon salt
   Black pepper to
   taste
½ cup mayonnaise
2 teaspoons lemon
   juice
½ cup cream of
   chicken soup,
   undiluted
1 cup (4 ounces)
   grated Cheddar
   cheese
1 cup crushed potato
   chips

Combine chicken, mushrooms, celery, onion, green pepper, almonds, salt and black pepper. Stir in mayonnaise, lemon juice and soup, mixing thoroughly. Pour mixture into buttered 2½-quart casserole. Sprinkle cheese and chips on chicken mixture. Bake at 350° for 30 minutes. Yield: 8 servings.

Plentiful "P's" Salad

Salad
- 4 16-ounce cans blackeyed peas, rinsed and drained
- 4 slices pepperoni, chopped
- 2 cups cooked rotini pasta
- 1 medium-sized red bell pepper, chopped
- 1 medium-sized green bell pepper, chopped
- 1 2-ounce jar pimiento, chopped
- 1 medium-sized purple onion, chopped
- 1 4½-ounce jar mushrooms, drained and chopped
- 2 tablespoons chopped parsley
- 4 slices provolone cheese, chopped

Combine peas, pepperoni, pasta, red and green peppers, pimiento, purple onion, mushrooms, parsley and cheese. Pour dressing over vegetables, tossing lightly but thoroughly. Chill, covered, for at least 2 hours before serving. Yield: 8 to 10 servings.

Dressing
- 1 envelope Italian salad dressing mix
- ½ teaspoon salt
- ¼ teaspoon black pepper
- ½ cup wine vinegar
- ¼ cup sugar
- ¼ cup vegetable oil

Combine salad dressing mix, salt and black pepper. Add vinegar and sugar, mixing well. Stir in oil. Pour dressing over vegetable mixture.

Tumi Salad

Salad

   3 **pounds chicken, cooked, boned, skin removed and diced**
   5 **tablespoons sesame seeds, toasted**
   5 **tablespoons almonds, sliced and toasted**
   ½ **head cabbage, thinly sliced**
   6 **green onions, sliced**
2½ **3-ounce packages chicken-flavored ramen noodles, crushed**
   1 **4-ounce can sliced black olives, drained**
   2 **cups sliced celery**

Combine chicken, sesame seeds, almonds, cabbage, onion, noodles, olives and celery in salad bowl. Pour dressing over chicken mixture, stirring thoroughly. Chill overnight. Yield: 8 to 10 servings.

Dressing

   3 **seasoning envelopes from ramen noodles**
   2 **tablespoons sugar**
   2 **teaspoons salt**
   ½ **teaspoon black pepper**
   1 **teaspoon seasoned salt**
   1 **cup canola oil**
   1 **cup cider vinegar**

Combine seasoning, sugar, salt, black pepper, seasoning salt, oil and vinegar in container with tightly-fitting lid. Shake until sugar and salt is dissolved. Pour dressing over salad ingredients.

Simple Shrimp Salad

1 to 1½ cups chopped
  cooked shrimp
1 hard-cooked egg,
  chopped
1½ cups finely chopped
  celery
1 cup diced cooked
  potatoes (optional)
2 teaspoons grated
  onion
¾ teaspoon salt
½ teaspoon curry
  powder
2 tablespoons lemon
  juice
½ cup mayonnaise

Combine shrimp, egg, celery, potatoes, onion, salt and curry powder. Add lemon juice and mayonnaise, mixing lightly but thoroughly. Chill. Serve on lettuce leaves. Yield: 3 to 4 servings.

Tuna Shell Salad

2½ cups small shell
  macaroni, cooked
  and drained
2 6⅛-ounce cans
  tuna, drained
1 cup chopped celery
½ cup chopped green
  bell pepper
½ cup sliced radishes
3 hard-cooked eggs,
  chopped
1 cup chopped
  walnuts
½ cup mayonnaise

Combine macaroni, tuna, celery, green pepper, radishes, eggs and walnuts. Add mayonnaise, mixing lightly but thoroughly. Yield: 8 to 10 servings.

NOT BY BREAD ALONE

Taffy Apple Salad

1 8-ounce can
   crushed pineapple,
   drained and juice
   reserved
½ cup sugar
1 tablespoon all-
   purpose flour
2 tablespoons cider
   vinegar
1 egg, beaten
1 8-ounce carton
   frozen whipped
   topping, thawed
2 cups salted Spanish
   peanuts
4 cups chopped
   unpeeled apples

Combine pineapple juice, sugar, flour and vinegar in saucepan. Add egg, blending well. Cook over medium heat, stirring frequently, until thickened. Let stand until cool. Fold topping, peanuts and apples into sauce. Yield: 12 to 16 servings.

Banana Salad

2 3-ounce packages
   cream cheese,
   softened
1 tablespoon lemon
   juice
2 tablespoons
   mayonnaise
½ teaspoon salt
2 tablespoons
   crushed pineapple
½ cup sliced
   maraschino
   cherries
½ cup chopped
   walnuts
1 cup whipping
   cream, whipped
3 bananas, diced

Combine cream cheese, lemon juice, mayonnaise and salt, beating until smooth. Add pineapple, cherries and walnuts, mixing thoroughly. Fold in whipped cream and bananas. Spread fruit mixture in large freezer-proof pan or dish. Freeze until firm. Yield: 8 to 12 servings.

Frosted Blueberry Salad

Salad

Dissolve gelatin in boiling water in shallow serving dish. Add undrained blueberries and pineapple. Add vinegar, stirring until well mixed. Chill until firm. Spread topping on firm salad. Chill, covered, until ready to serve. Yield: 6 to 8 servings.

- 1 6-ounce package raspberry gelatin
- 1 cup boiling water
- 1 15-ounce can blueberries with syrup
- 1 8-ounce can crushed pineapple with juice
- 1 tablespoon white vinegar

Topping

Combine cream cheese and sugar, beating until smooth. Add vanilla and sour cream, blending thoroughly. Spread cream mixture on firm salad.

- 1 8-ounce package cream cheese, softened
- ¼ cup sugar
- 1 cup sour cream
- 1 teaspoon vanilla

Cranberry Gelatin Salad

Combine pineapple juice with water to measure 1 cup. Pour into saucepan and bring to a boil. Add gelatin and stir until dissolved. Stir in 1 cup cold water. Chill until thickened. Add cranberry sauce, pineapple, celery and pecans. Chill until firm. Yield: 8 to 10 servings.

- 1 13-ounce can crushed or tidbit pineapple, drained and juice reserved
- Water
- 1 6-ounce package cherry gelatin
- 1 cup cold water
- 1 16-ounce can whole cranberry sauce
- 1 cup chopped celery
- ½ cup chopped pecans

Mixed Fruit Salad

1 16-ounce can sliced peaches
1 20-ounce can pineapple chunks
2 20-ounce cans mandarin oranges
1 3¼-ounce package vanilla tapioca pudding mix
1 3⅛-ounce package vanilla pudding mix

Drain peaches, pineapple and oranges, reserving juice. Combine 3 cups juice and pudding mixes in saucepan. Cook over medium heat until thickened or prepare using microwave according to package directions. Let sauce stand until cool. Pour sauce over fruit, adding others such as banana chunks, cherries or grapes, if desired. Serve with pound cake. Yield: 12 servings.

Grapefruit Gelatin Salad

1 16-ounce can grapefruit segments, drained and juice reserved
Water
1 3-ounce package lime gelatin
1 tablespoon lime or lemon juice
¼ teaspoon salt
1 cup cold evaporated milk
½ cup chopped pecans
½ cup chopped celery

Measure 1¼ cups grapefruit juice, adding water if necessary, in saucepan. Bring to a boil. Add gelatin and stir until dissolved. Add lime or lemon juice and salt. Chill gelatin until partially thickened. Cut grapefruit segments into small pieces. Add grapefruit, milk, pecans and celery to gelatin, mixing thoroughly. Salad may be frozen. Yield: 4 to 6 servings.

Lime Party Salad

Combine marshmallows and milk in top of double boiler. Cook over moderately-boiling water until marshmallows are melted. Prepare gelatin according to package directions. Pour hot marshmallow liquid into gelatin, stirring until dissolved. Add cream cheese, mixing well. Stir in pineapple with juice. Let stand until cool. Fold in whipping cream and mayonnaise, mixing lightly but thoroughly. Chill until firm. Yield: 10 to 12 servings.

- ¼ pound marshmallows
- 1 cup milk
- 1 3-ounce package lime gelatin
- 2 3-ounce packages cream cheese, cubed
- 1 16-ounce can crushed pineapple, undrained
- 1 cup whipping cream, whipped
- ⅔ cup mayonnaise

Strawberry Gelatin Salad

Dissolve gelatin in boiling water. Add strawberries, pineapple, bananas and pecans. Pour ½ of gelatin mixture into serving bowl or container large enough to contain all of mixture. Chill until firm; do not refrigerate remaining gelatin mixture. Using electric mixer, beat sour cream, cream cheese and sugar together until smooth. Spread creamed mixture on firm gelatin. Pour remaining gelatin mixture over cream layer. Chill until firm. Yield: 6 to 8 servings.

- 1 6-ounce package strawberry gelatin
- 1 cup boiling water
- 1 8-ounce package frozen strawberries, partially thawed
- 1 8-ounce can crushed pineapple
- 2 bananas, mashed
- ½ to ¾ cup chopped pecans
- 1 cup sour cream
- 1 3-ounce package cream cheese, softened
- 2 tablespoons sugar

NOT BY BREAD ALONE

Pretzel Salad

Crust

>   2 cups broken
>   pretzels
>   1 cup margarine,
>   melted

Combine pretzels and margarine. Press evenly in bottom of 13x9x2-inch baking pan. Bake at 350° for 15 minutes. Let stand until cool.

Filling

>   1 8-ounce package
>   cream cheese,
>   softened
>   1 cup sugar
>   1 9-ounce carton
>   frozen whipped
>   topping, thawed
>   1 16-ounce can
>   crushed pineapple,
>   drained and 1 cup
>   juice reserved
>   1 cup water
>   1 6-ounce package
>   strawberry gelatin
>   2 10-ounce packages
>   frozen strawberries,
>   partially thawed

Combine cream cheese and sugar, beating until smooth. Fold in whipped topping. Spread creamed mixture on pretzel crust. Combine pineapple juice and water in saucepan. Bring to a boil. Add gelatin, stirring until dissolved. Add strawberries and pineapple to gelatin mixture. Cool until partially thickened, then spoon evenly on cream layer. Chill. Yield: 16 to 20 servings.

Buttermilk Salad Dressing Mix

Mix

- 2¼ **cups powdered buttermilk**
- ¾ **cup freeze-dried chives**
- ¼ **cup dill weed**
- ¼ **cup sugar or sugar substitute**
- 2 **tablespoons dry mustard**

Combine buttermilk, chives, dill, sugar and mustard, mixing thoroughly. Store in 1-quart jar, tightly covered, in refrigerator. Yield: 3⅔ cups.

Dressing

- 5 **tablespoons dressing mix**
- ½ **cup warm water**
- 2 **tablespoons cider vinegar**
- 1 **tablespoon sour cream**

Combine ingredients, whisking to blend thoroughly.

Ranch Style Salad Dressing

- 1 **cup buttermilk**
- 1 **cup mayonnaise (not salad dressing)**
- 2 **teaspoons chopped parsley**
- ½ **teaspoon onion powder**
- 1 **teaspoon garlic powder**
- 2 **teaspoons seasoned salt**
- 2 **teaspoons salt**
- 1 **teaspoon black pepper**

Combine buttermilk and mayonnaise, mixing until smooth. Add parsley, onion powder, garlic powder, seasoned salt, salt and black pepper, blending well. Chill before using. Yield: 2 cups.

Herb Salad Dressing Mix

Mix

 ¼ **cup parsley flakes**
 2 **tablespoons dried oregano, crushed**
 2 **tablespoons basil leaves, crushed**
 2 **tablespoons marjoram, crushed**
 2 **tablespoons sugar or sugar substitute**
 1 **tablespoon fennel seeds, crushed**
 1 **tablespoon dry mustard**
 1½ **teaspoons black pepper**

Combine parsley, oregano, basil, marjoram, sugar, fennel, mustard and black pepper in 1-pint jar. Cover and shake well to mix. Store in cool, dark place. Yield: ¾ cup.

Dressing

 1 **tablespoon salad dressing mix**
 ¾ **cup warm water**
 2½ **tablespoons tarragon or white vinegar**
 1 **tablespoon olive oil**
 1 **clove garlic, crushed**

Combine salad dressing mix, water, vinegar, oil and garlic. Whisk to blend thoroughly. Check seasoning, adding ¼ to ½ teaspoon more herb mixture if desired. Let stand at room temperature for at least 30 minutes. Shake well before using. Yield: 1 cup.

Sweet and Sour Salad Dressing

Combine ketchup and vinegar. Combine Worcestershire sauce, salt, mustard and powdered sugar. Add to ketchup mixture, mixing thoroughly. Blend in oil. Yield: 1¼ cups.

Variation: Combine ⅓ cup dressing with ⅓ cup mayonnaise. Add chopped chives and crumbled blue cheese to taste.

¼ **cup ketchup**
¼ **cup garlic-flavored wine vinegar**
¼ **teaspoon Worcestershire sauce**
½ **teaspoon salt**
½ **teaspoon dry mustard**
2 **tablespoons powdered sugar**
¾ **cup vegetable oil**

Coleslaw Dressing

Combine egg yolks, sugar, dry mustard, salt and cayenne pepper in top of double boiler. Add oil. Cook over moderately-boiling water, stirring constantly, until thickened. Stir in vinegar and cook for a few more minutes. Remove from heat. Let stand until cool. Fold in sour cream. Yield: 2 cups.

3 **egg yolks, beaten**
½ **cup sugar**
1 **teaspoon dry mustard**
1 **teaspoon salt Cayenne pepper to taste**
¼ **cup vegetable oil**
½ **cup vinegar**
½ **cup sour cream**

Sweet and Crunchy Tuna Salad

1 can tuna, drained
1 4-ounce can
   pineapple tidbits
   (drained)
2 to 3 tablespoons
   sliced almonds or
   pecan pieces
½ celery stalk, diced
⅓ cup mayonnaise
   Salt and pepper to
   taste
1 teaspoon poppy
   seeds (optional)

Mix all ingredients together. Chill. Serve on toasted bread or croissants with lettuce and tomatoes.

Note: Chicken or turkey may be substituted for tuna.

COME & DINE

Wisdom. . .
has built her house;
she has hewn out its seven pillars.
She has prepared her meat and
mixed her wine;
she has also set her table.
She calls. . .
Come, and eat my food
and drink the wine I have mixed.
Leave your simple ways and you
will live; walk in the way
of understanding.

PROVERBS 9: 1-6

E   N   T   R   E   E   S

Mexican Beef

4 **pounds chuck roast**
   Salt and black
   pepper to taste
   Garlic powder to
   taste
   Chili powder to
   taste
   Cumin to taste
1 **4-ounce can**
   chopped green
   chilies
1 **29-ounce can whole**
   tomatoes

Generously season roast with salt, black pepper, garlic powder, chili powder and cumin. Place on sheet of heavy-duty aluminum foil and place in shallow roasting pan. Pour green chilies on roast and fold foil to enclose it. Bake in preheated oven at 250° for 8 hours or overnight. Remove fat and bone. Add tomatoes. Continue baking, with foil open, for 1 hour or until tender. Serve beef with warm flour tortillas or over rice. Yield: 8 to 12 servings.

Prime Rib

4 **to 6 pounds prime**
   rib
2 **tablespoons**
   Worcestershire
   sauce
   Salt and black
   pepper to taste
1 **teaspoon paprika**
   Rock salt
   Water

Season prime rib with Worcestershire sauce, salt, black pepper and paprika. Pour layer of rock salt into large heavy pan or roasting pan, completely covering bottom of pan. Lightly moisten rock salt with water. Place prime rib, in standing position, on rock salt. Cover completely with rock salt so that no prime rib is exposed. Lightly moisten rock salt with water. Bake in preheated oven at 500° for 12 minutes per pound. Remove from oven. Using wooden mallet or hammer, gently tap hard salt crust to create cracks and carefully pull salt pieces from prime rib. Yield: 12 to 16 servings.

Note: *Rock salt crust traps the juices of the prime rib and minimizes shrinkage without imparting a salty flavor to it.*

Pastrami

Place brisket in large heavy pot with water to cover. Add garlic and bay leaves. Simmer, covered, for 4 hours or until tender. Drain and let stand until cool. Brush all surfaces of brisket with liquid smoke. Combine black pepper, allspice and coriander. Sprinkle seasoning mixture on all surfaces of brisket. Bake, covered, at 350° for 45 minutes. Cool before slicing. Yield: 16 to 20 servings.

5 pounds corned beef brisket
Water
2 cloves garlic
3 bay leaves
Liquid smoke
1½ teaspoons black pepper
¾ teaspoon allspice
½ teaspoon coriander

Broccoli and Beef Casserole

Sauté beef and mushrooms until beef is browned. Drain excess fat. Prepare broccoli according to package directions, cooking until just tender. Drain well. Add broccoli, sour cream, soup, onion, black pepper and garlic salt to beef mixture, mixing thoroughly. Pour ½ of mixture into 2-quart casserole. Sprinkle 1 cup of cheese on beef mixture. Repeat layers. Bake, uncovered, at 350° for 35 to 45 minutes or until cheese is lightly browned. Yield: 4 to 6 servings.

1 pound ground beef
1 8-ounce can mushrooms or 1 cup sliced fresh mushrooms
2 10-ounce packages frozen chopped broccoli
1 cup sour cream
1 10¾-ounce can cream of celery soup, undiluted
5 teaspoons minced onion
½ teaspoon black pepper
1 teaspoon garlic salt
2 cups (8 ounces) grated mozzarella cheese

Steak with Mushroom Brown Sauce

Steak
    2 tablespoons lemon
        juice
    2 tablespoons
        molasses
    2 tablespoons
        Worcestershire
        sauce
    1 teaspoon seasoned
        pepper
    ½ teaspoon seasoned
        salt or Creole
        seasoning
    2 pounds boneless
        sirloin steak

Combine lemon juice, molasses, Worcestershire sauce, pepper and salt. Pour into large shallow dish. Add steak. Chill, covered, for at least 1 hour, turning once. Drain steak, reserving marinade. Grill steak over hot coals for 8 to 12 minutes on each side or to desired doneness, basting frequently with reserved marinade. Spoon Mushroom Brown Sauce over steak. Yield: 4 to 6 servings.

Mushroom Brown Sauce
    4 thin slices onion
    3½ tablespoons butter
        or margarine,
        divided
    1½ tablespoons all-
        purpose flour
    1 teaspoon beef
        bouillon granules
    1 cup water
    ½ cup sliced
        mushrooms
    ⅛ teaspoon black
        pepper

Sauté onion in 1½ tablespoons butter in heavy skillet until onion is tender. Discard onion. Cook butter over low heat until it begins to brown. Add flour, stirring until smooth. Cook for 1 minute, stirring constantly. Add bouillon granules and gradually add water. Cook, stirring constantly, over medium heat until thickened and bubbly. Sauté mushrooms in 2 table-spoons butter until tender. Drain and add to sauce. Add black pepper. Serve sauce over steak.

Beefy Mushroom Pie

Melt 1 tablespoon shortening in skillet on medium heat. Add beef, chopped peppers and onion; sauté 3 to 5 minutes. Add undiluted soup and next 6 ingredients. Reduce heat to low; cover and simmer 20 minutes. Preheat oven to 375°. Place pie crust on bottom of 9-inch pie plate. Combine cornstarch and water. Stir into hot beef filling. Pour into unbaked pie shell. Top with cooked potatoes. Melt remaining 1 teaspoon shortening; brush onto filled pie. Top with pie crust. Trim ½-inch beyond edge of pie plate. Fold top edge under bottom crust. Flute. Brush crust with beaten egg. Cut slits in top crust so steam can escape. Bake for 45 minutes or until filling is bubbly and crust is a light golden brown. Let stand for 5 minutes. Serve hot.

1 tablespoon plus 1 teaspoon butter-flavor shortening
3 cups cubed, cooked roast beef (1 pound), or 1 pound roast beef from deli, cubed
¼ cup green pepper
¼ cup red pepper
¼ cup chopped onion
1 10¾-ounce can condensed beefy mushroom soup
1 4.5-ounce can sliced or chopped mushrooms, drained
¼ teaspoon salt-free seasoning mix
¼ teaspoon garlic salt Pinch of ground black pepper
1 teaspoon Worcestershire sauce
2 tablespoons cornstarch
2 tablespoons water
2 cups sliced, cooked potatoes (1 pound raw) Pie crust for double crust, 9-inch pie

Burgundy Beef Tips

4 slices bacon
1½ pounds beef round
　steak, cut in 1½-
　inch cubes
1 10¾-ounce can
　golden mushroom
　soup, undiluted
½ cup burgundy
2 tablespoons parsley
⅛ teaspoon black
　pepper
½ cup water
¾ pound small white
　onions
2 cups sliced
　mushrooms

Sauté bacon until crisp. Remove from skillet, drain and crumble bacon. Sauté beef in bacon drippings. Remove excess fat. Add soup, burgundy, parsley, black pepper and water to beef. Simmer, covered, for 1½ hours. Add onions, mushrooms and bacon. Continue cooking, covered, for 1 hour. Serve beef tips on wide noodles or rice. Yield: 6 servings.

Saucy Little Meat Loaves

1½ pounds ground
　round of beef
¾ cup uncooked
　rolled oats
¼ cup chopped onion
1 egg, beaten
¾ cup milk
1½ teaspoons salt
¼ teaspoon black
　pepper
⅓ cup ketchup
1 tablespoon
　prepared mustard
1 tablespoon brown
　sugar

Combine beef, oats, onion, egg, milk, salt and black pepper. Shape mixture into 6 loaves and place in shallow baking pan. Combine ketchup, mustard and brown sugar. Spread sauce on loaves. Bake at 350° for 35 to 40 minutes. Yield: 6 servings.

Note: Loaves may be frozen, enclosed in aluminum foil, before or after baking.

Stuffed Shells

Combine ricotta, mozzarella and
Parmesan cheese, eggs and parsley. Set
aside.

Sauté beef with onion and garlic until
browned. Drain excess fat. Place
tomatoes in blender container and
process until smooth. Add tomatoes,
tomato paste, sugar, salt, black pepper,
oregano and basil to beef. Simmer for
1 hour. Prepare shells according to
package directions and drain well.
Spoon cheese filling into shells. Pour
small amount of meat sauce into
13x9x2-inch baking pan. Place stuffed
shells on sauce and pour remaining
sauce over shells. Sprinkle with
Parmesan cheese. Bake, covered with
aluminum foil, at 350° for 25 minutes.
Yield: 8 servings.

Filling
- 2 16-ounce cartons ricotta cheese
- 2 cups (8 ounces) grated mozzarella cheese
- ½ cup (2 ounces) grated Parmesan cheese
- 2 eggs
- 1 tablespoon chopped parsley

Sauce
- 2 pounds ground beef
- 2 medium-sized onions, minced
- 2 cloves garlic, minced
- 2 16-ounce cans tomatoes
- 1 6-ounce can tomato paste
- 3 tablespoons sugar
  Salt and black pepper to taste
- ½ teaspoon oregano
- ¼ teaspoon basil
- 1 16-ounce package jumbo pasta shells
  Grated Parmesan cheese

Spaghetti Pie

1 pound ground beef
1 medium-sized onion, chopped
1 medium-sized green bell pepper, chopped
1 6-ounce can tomato paste
1 8-ounce can tomatoes, crushed
Salt and black pepper to taste
Garlic to taste
1 6-ounce package spaghetti, cooked and drained
2 eggs
¾ cup (3 ounces) grated Parmesan cheese, divided
1 12-ounce carton cottage cheese

Sauté beef until browned, drain and crumble. Add onion, green pepper, tomato paste, tomatoes, salt, black pepper and garlic. Simmer for 30 minutes. Combine spaghetti, eggs and ½ cup Parmesan cheese. Pour spaghetti mixture into buttered 9-inch pie pan. Spread cottage cheese on spaghetti. Add meat mixture on cottage cheese layer. Bake at 350° for 30 minutes. Sprinkle with ¼ cup Parmesan cheese. Yield: 6 servings.

Shepherd's Pie

1 pound ground beef
1 onion, minced
1 carrot, diced
Garlic to taste
Black pepper to taste
6 large potatoes

Sauté beef until browned. Drain excess fat. Add onion, carrot, garlic and black pepper. Simmer until onion is tender. Cook potatoes until tender, drain and mash. Spread meat mixture in 8x8x2-inch baking dish. Spoon potatoes on meat mixture. Bake at 350° for 25 to 35 minutes or until bubbly and potatoes are lightly browned and crusted. Yield: 4 to 6 servings.

Pasticchio

Prepare pasta according to package directions. Drain well. Add egg, milk and Parmesan cheese. Set aside. Sauté beef and onion until beef is lightly browned and onion is tender. Drain excess fat. Add tomato sauce, salt, black pepper, cinnamon and nutmeg. Set aside. Prepare sauce. Layer ½ of pasta in 8x8x2-inch baking pan. Spoon meat mixture on pasta and top with remaining pasta. Pour cream sauce over pasta. Bake at 350° for 45 to 50 minutes. Let stand 10 minutes before serving. Yield: 4 to 6 servings.

1½ **cups uncooked mostaccioli or mezzeni pasta**
1 **egg, beaten**
¼ **cup milk, divided**
⅓ **cup (3 ounces) grated Parmesan cheese**
1 **pound ground beef**
½ **cup chopped onion**
1 **8-ounce can tomato sauce**
¾ **teaspoon salt**
⅛ **teaspoon black pepper**
½ **teaspoon cinnamon**
⅛ **teaspoon nutmeg**

Cream Sauce
3 **tablespoons butter**
3 **tablespoons all-purpose flour**
¼ **teaspoon salt**
½ **cup milk**
1 **egg, beaten**
¼ **cup (1 ounce) grated Parmesan cheese**

Melt butter in saucepan. Blend in flour and salt. Add milk. Cook, stirring frequently, until thickened and bubbly. Continue cooking for 1 minute. Blend small amount of hot mixture with egg, then add egg mixture to sauce in pan. Stir in cheese.

Italian Spaghetti

Meatballs

   6 slices day-old bread
     Milk
   2 pounds ground beef
   1 pound ground pork
   1 egg, lightly beaten
   1 green bell pepper,
     chopped
   5 or 6 cloves garlic,
     minced
  ¼ cup (1 ounce)
     grated Parmesan
     cheese
     Salt and black
     pepper to taste
   1 tablespoon basil
  ½ teaspoon oregano
  ½ teaspoon parsley
     flakes
  ½ teaspoon thyme
     Cayenne pepper to
     taste
  ½ cup vegetable oil

Soak bread in milk, drain and press to remove excess moisture. Combine bread, beef, pork, egg, green pepper, garlic, cheese, salt, black pepper, basil, oregano, parsley flakes, thyme and cayenne pepper, mixing well. Shape into 1½-inch balls. Sauté meatballs in oil, turning to brown on all sides. Reserve 2 tablespoons pan drippings for sauce. Simmer meatballs, covered, during sauce preparation.

*(Italian Spaghetti,
continued on next page)*

(Italian Spaghetti, continued)

*Combine tomato paste, water, juice,
meat drippings, green pepper, garlic,
salt, black pepper, basil, cayenne
pepper and pepperoni in large saucepan. Add browned meatballs. Simmer
for 3 hours or longer, stirring occasionally. Yield: 12 servings.*

Sauce
- **3 or 4 6-ounce cans tomato paste**
- **3 or 4 cans water**
- **4 cups tomato juice**
- **2 tablespoons meat drippings**
- **½ green bell pepper, chopped**
- **5 or 6 cloves garlic, minced**
  Salt and black pepper to taste
- **1 tablespoon basil**
  Cayenne pepper to taste (optional)
  Pepperoni stick, sliced

Sloppy Joes

- **2 pounds ground beef**
- **1 onion, chopped**
- **1 cup ketchup**
- **½ cup water**
- **½ teaspoon vinegar**
- **½ teaspoon Worcestershire sauce**
- **1 teaspoon brown sugar**
- **1 teaspoon prepared mustard**
- **½ teaspoon chili powder**

*Sauté beef and onion until beef is
browned. Drain excess fat. Add
ketchup, water, vinegar,
Worcestershire sauce, brown sugar,
mustard and chili powder to beef
mixture. Simmer for 15 to 20 minutes.
Serve in pita bread halves with cheese
and/or lettuce. Yield: 8 servings.*

Korean Pork Strip

3 pounds pork
   tenderloin
¼ teaspoon cayenne
   pepper
2½ tablespoons sugar
⅓ cup soy sauce
¼ cup chopped onion
4 cloves garlic,
   minced
2 tablespoons sesame
   seed, toasted
½ teaspoon ginger

Season pork with cayenne pepper and sprinkle with sugar. Combine soy sauce, onion, garlic, sesame seed and ginger in glass dish. Add pork. Marinate for several hours or overnight. Broil or grill pork until done. Yield: 6 to 8 servings.

Note: Marinade may be used with chicken.

Pork Tenderloin with Wine Sauce

2 teaspoons all-
   purpose flour
   Salt and black
   pepper to taste
1 10 to 12-ounce pork
   tenderloin, trimmed
   and cut in 1-inch
   slices
2 tablespoons
   margarine
2 tablespoons olive
   oil
1 large shallot,
   chopped
½ cup sliced fresh
   mushrooms
⅛ teaspoon dried
   rosemary, crushed
¼ cup dry white wine
¼ cup chicken broth

Combine flour, salt and black pepper in plastic bag. Place pork in bag and shake to cover with seasoned flour. Melt margarine and oil in large heavy skillet over medium heat. Add pork and cook for 2 minutes. Add shallot and continue cooking for 3 minutes, turning pork to lightly brown both sides. Stir in mushrooms and rosemary. Add wine and broth. Simmer for about 3 minutes or until pork is thoroughly cooked. Serve over rice or pasta with pan liquid. Yield: 2 to 4 servings.

Pork Chops
Modenese

**4 1-inch thick loin
    pork chops**
¼ cup margarine
½ cup dry white wine
**2 cloves garlic,
    minced**
1 teaspoon salt
**⅛ teaspoon black
    pepper**
**1 teaspoon dried
    rosemary, crushed**
1 teaspoon dried sage
**2 tablespoons lemon
    juice**

*Sauté pork in margarine in large
skillet, turning to brown on both sides.
Add wine, garlic, salt, black pepper,
rosemary and sage. Simmer, covered,
for about 20 minutes or until pork is
tender, turning once. Remove pork to
warm platter. Stir lemon juice into pan
liquid and simmer for 1 minute. Pour
sauce over pork. Serve with pasta and
grated Parmesan cheese. Yield: 4
servings.*

Pork Chops
Supreme

**6 to 8 pork chops, fat
    trimmed**
1 onion, sliced
**1 lemon, sliced
    Brown sugar**
**6 to 8 tablespoons
    ketchup**

*Place pork chops in single layer in
baking dish. Place onion slice and
lemon slice on each and generously
sprinkle with brown sugar. Spoon 1
tablespoon ketchup on each pork chop.
Bake, covered, at 350° for 1 hour;
remove cover and continue baking for
30 minutes, basting a few times with
liquid from baking dish. Yield: 6 to 8
servings.*

Pork and Vegetables

3 or 4 pork chops
Salt and black
pepper to taste
1 tablespoon
vegetable oil
¾ pound new
potatoes, cut in
halves
1 cup water
2 16-ounce cans green
beans, undrained
½ teaspoon dried sage

Season pork chops with salt and black pepper. Sauté pork chops in oil in skillet, turning to brown on both sides. Place potatoes on pork chops and add water. Simmer, covered, for 20 minutes. Add green beans with liquid and sage. Season with salt and black pepper. Simmer, covered, for 20 minutes or until potatoes are tender. Yield: 3 or 4 servings.

Zucchini Sausage Bake

1 pound Italian bulk
sausage
5 tablespoons all-
purpose flour,
divided
6 cups sliced zucchini
½ cup chopped onion
2 tablespoons
margarine or butter
2 cups cottage cheese
¼ cup (1 ounce)
grated Parmesan or
Romano cheese
2 eggs, well beaten
½ teaspoon garlic salt
1 cup (4 ounces)
shredded Cheddar
cheese

Sauté sausage in large skillet, stirring to crumble, until browned. Drain excess fat. Add 1 tablespoon flour, tossing to blend with sausage. Spread sausage in 11x9x2-inch baking dish. Sauté zucchini and onion in margarine until tender but not browned. Remove from heat and add ¼ cup flour, tossing to blend with vegetables. Spread ½ of squash mixture on sausage. Combine cottage cheese, grated cheese, eggs and garlic salt. Spoon cheese mixture on squash layer. Spread remaining squash mixture on cheese. Bake at 350° for 30 to 35 minutes. Sprinkle with Cheddar cheese and continue baking for 2 minutes. Yield: 6 to 8 servings.

South Texas Venison Stew

Dredge venison in flour to coat thoroughly. Sauté venison, carrots, onion and garlic in oil until partially tender. Stir in soup, broth, black pepper, bay leaf, seasoning and thyme. Simmer, partially covered, for 1½ to 2 hours. Remove bay leaf. Yield: 6 servings.

Variation: Potatoes or rice may be cooked in stew. Add broth to prevent sticking.

- 1½ to 2½ pounds venison, cut in bite-sized pieces
- 2 cups all-purpose flour
- 2 large carrots, sliced
- 1 medium-sized onion, sliced
- 2 cloves garlic, minced
- Vegetable oil
- 1 10¾-ounce can cream of golden mushroom soup, undiluted
- 4 cups beef broth
- ⅛ teaspoon black pepper
- 1 bay leaf
- 2 teaspoons all-purpose seasoning
- 1½ teaspoons thyme

Chicken Oriental

Combine soy sauce, butter, garlic, paprika, curry powder, cinnamon and ginger. Add chicken to sauce and sprinkle with sesame seed. Let stand for 1 hour. Bake, uncovered, at 250° for 2 hours. Yield: 4 servings.

- ¼ cup soy sauce
- 2 to 3 tablespoons melted butter
- 1 clove garlic, crushed
- 1 tablespoon paprika
- 1 tablespoon curry powder
- 1 teaspoon cinnamon
- 1 teaspoon ginger
- 4 chicken breast halves
- Sesame seed

Chinatown Chicken

2 cups sliced
   mushrooms
3 tablespoons
   vegetable oil
2 cups sliced celery
1 large green bell
   pepper, cut in
   chunks
8 chicken breast
   halves, skin
   removed, boned and
   cut in ½-inch
   chunks
1 16-ounce can
   pineapple tidbits,
   drained and liquid
   reserved
½ cup dry sherry
¼ cup soy sauce
1 teaspoon garlic salt
½ teaspoon ginger
2 tablespoons
   cornstarch
½ cup sliced green
   onion

Sauté mushrooms in oil, tossing until golden. Add celery and green pepper. Cook for 2 to 3 minutes. Stir in chicken and cook for about 15 minutes or until chicken is creamy white. Combine pineapple juice, sherry, soy sauce, garlic salt, ginger and cornstarch. Add to chicken and vegetables and cook until thickened. Fold in pineapple and green onion. Serve with rice. Yield: 8 servings.

Apricot Chicken

Season chicken with salt and black pepper. Sprinkle with flour. Sauté chicken in margarine in large skillet, turning to brown on both sides, until nearly done. Place chicken in shallow baking dish. Sauté celery and onion in pan drippings until vegetables are tender. Spoon apricots and vegetables on chicken in dish. Combine reserved apricot liquid, soy sauce and ginger in skillet and bring to a boil. Pour sauce over chicken. Bake at 350° for 20 minutes or until thoroughly heated. Yield: 4 servings.

4 chicken breast halves, skin removed, boned and flattened
Salt and black pepper to taste
All-purpose flour
2 tablespoons margarine or butter
½ cup chopped celery
1 small onion, sliced
1 17-ounce can apricot halves, drained and ½ cup liquid reserved
1 tablespoon soy sauce
¼ teaspoon ginger

Chicken Diane

Prepare pasta according to package directions. Combine chicken and chicken seasoning. Sauté chicken in ¼ cup margarine for about 4 minutes, stirring frequently. Add mushrooms and stir-fry for 2 minutes. Add onion, parsley and garlic, mixing well. Stir in broth and cook for 2 minutes or until sauce is bubbly. Add ¼ cup margarine and cook for 3 minutes. Stir in cooked and drained pasta, mixing thoroughly. Yield: 4 servings.

1 6-ounce package spaghetti
¾ pound boneless, skinless chicken breasts, cut in strips
5 teaspoons spicy chicken seasoning
½ cup margarine, divided
½ pound fresh mushrooms, sliced
2 green onions, sliced
2 tablespoons minced parsley
1 teaspoon minced garlic
1 cup chicken broth

Chicken Avocado Melt

4 **chicken breast halves, skin removed, boned and flattened**
2 **tablespoons cornstarch**
1 **teaspoon ground cumin**
2 **teaspoons garlic salt or powder**
1 **egg, lightly beaten**
1 **tablespoon water**
⅓ **cup cornmeal**
3 **tablespoons vegetable oil**
1 **firm ripe avocado, peeled and sliced**
1½ **cups (6 ounces) shredded Monterey Jack cheese**
½ **cup sour cream**
¼ **cup sliced green onion tops**
¼ **cup chopped red or green bell pepper**
2 **cherry tomatoes, cut in halves (optional)**
Parsley sprigs (optional)

Dredge chicken in mixture of cornstarch, cumin and garlic, coating each piece thoroughly. Combine egg and water. Dip chicken into egg liquid, then in cornmeal, coating evenly. Sauté chicken in oil in large skillet over medium heat, cooking for 2 minutes on each side. Place chicken in baking dish. Place avocado slices on chicken. Sprinkle with cheese. Bake at 350° for 15 minutes or until chicken is fork tender and cheese is melted. Spoon dollop of sour cream on each chicken piece. Sprinkle with onion and bell pepper and garnish with tomatoes and parsley. Yield: 4 servings.

Birds Nest Chicken

Season chicken breasts with salt and pepper. Place chicken in a 13x9-inch baking dish sprayed with non-stick cooking spray. Spoon mushrooms and spinach over chicken. Arrange pasta over chicken. Bring soup and milk to a boil, stirring constantly. Pour over pasta, covering all the pasta and chicken. Bake at 375° for one hour. Add cheese to top of dish and bake for 5 more minutes.

- 8 **nests of angel hair pasta**
- 8 **chicken breasts halves, skinned and boned**
- 6 **ounces mushrooms**
- 1 **package frozen, chopped spinach**
- 2 **cans cream of chicken soup**
- 1 **can milk**
- 3 **ounces each of Monterey Jack and Cheddar cheese**
  Salt and pepper to taste

Chicken with Fruit

Sauté chicken in oil until browned on all sides. Combine orange juice, honey, lemon juice, salt and curry powder. Dip chicken in sauce and arrange in baking dish. Pour sauce over chicken. Bake, uncovered, at 350° for 25 minutes. Turn chicken and add 1 or more kinds of fruit. Baste fruit with sauce. Continue baking for 45 minutes or until chicken is tender. Yield: 3 or 4 servings.

- 3 to 4 **pounds chicken pieces**
  Vegetable oil
- 1 **cup orange juice**
- ¼ **cup honey**
- 2 **tablespoons lemon juice**
- 1 **teaspoon salt**
- 1½ **teaspoons curry powder**
  Kumquats
  Peaches
  Pears
  Prunes
  Apricots
  Raisins
  Strips of orange peel

Arroz Con Pollo

(Cuban Style Chicken with Rice)

3 to 4 pounds chicken
   pieces
   Salt and black
   pepper to taste
   Paprika to taste
1 large onion,
   chopped
1 small green bell
   pepper, chopped
2 small cloves garlic,
   minced
1 2-ounce jar
   pimiento, drained
   and diced
¼ to ½ teaspoon chili
   powder
2 chicken bouillon
   cubes
¼ to ½ pound cooked
   pork sausage or 1
   cup diced ham
1 28-ounce can
   tomatoes, crushed
1 3-ounce jar
   pimiento-stuffed
   green olives
1 cup dry wine or any
   cooking wine
1 teaspoon sarzon
   (Spanish spice)
1 cup uncooked
   regular rice
1 10-ounce package
   frozen peas

Season chicken with salt, black pepper and paprika. Combine chicken, onion, green pepper, garlic, pimiento, chili powder, bouillon, meat, tomatoes, olives, wine and sarzon in slow cooker. Cook, covered, at low setting for 6 to 8 hours. Add rice and peas. Cook, covered, at high setting for 1 to 2 hours or until rice is tender, stirring occasionally. Yield: 3 or 4 servings.

Chicken and Noodles

Cook chicken, seasoned with salt, black pepper and parsley, in 1¾ quarts water for 1½ hours. Remove chicken from broth, remove skin and bone and cut into bite-sized pieces. Reserve 1½ quarts broth. Beat egg and yolks until light. Add water and salt, beating well. Stir in 2 cups flour and mix by hand. Divide dough in two portions. Roll to ¹⁄₁₆-inch thickness and cut in strips. Place on wax paper with 3 to 4 table-spoons flour and cover. Let dry. Bring broth to a boil. Add noodles and cook for 20 minutes. Add chicken and cook for 5 minutes. Yield: 6 to 8 servings.

3 to 4 pounds chicken, cut up
Salt and black pepper to taste
Parsley
1¾ quarts water
1 egg
3 egg yolks
3 tablespoons cold water
1 teaspoon salt
2 cups sifted all-purpose flour
All-purpose flour

Chicken Pot Pie

Sauté onion and celery in butter in saucepan until vegetables are tender. Place pastry for 1 crust in 9-inch deep dish pie pan. Bake at 325° for 2 to 3 minutes, remove and gently spread pastry to edge of pan. Combine onion-celery mixture, soup, chicken, cheese, peas and carrots and mushrooms. Pour chicken mixture into pastry shell. Top with remaining pastry, crimping edges to seal and cutting several slits in crust to vent steam. Bake at 325° for 45 minutes, broiling for last few minutes to brown crust. Yield: 6 servings.

¼ cup minced onion
½ cup diced celery
2 tablespoons butter
Pastry for double-crust 9-inch pie
2 10¾-ounce cans cream of chicken soup, undiluted
2 cups cubed cooked chicken
1 cup (4 ounces) grated American cheese
1 16-ounce can peas and carrots, drained
1 4-ounce can sliced mushrooms, drained

Chicken Quiche

¼ **cup chopped onion**
2 **tablespoons butter**
3 **eggs**
1 **envelope chicken**
   gravy mix
1 **cup milk**
2 **cups diced cooked**
   chicken
1 **9-inch unbaked**
   pastry shell
1 **cup (4 ounces)**
   shredded Cheddar
   cheese

Sauté onion in butter until tender. Combine eggs, gravy mix and milk, beating well. Stir in chicken and onion. Pour chicken mixture into pastry shell. Sprinkle cheese on chicken mixture. Bake at 375° for 25 minutes or until knife tip inserted near center comes out clean. Let stand about 10 minutes before serving. Yield: 6 servings.

Chicken Spaghetti

2½ **to 3 pound chicken,**
   cut up
   Water
   Salt and black
   pepper
1 **16-ounce package**
   spaghetti
1 **small onion, diced**
   Garlic to taste
1 **tablespoon butter**
1 **10¾-ounce can**
   cream of mushroom
   soup, undiluted
1 **10¾-ounce can**
   cream of chicken
   soup, undiluted
1 **16-ounce can**
   stewed tomatoes
1 **16-ounce package**
   pasteurized process
   cheese spread,
   cubed

Place chicken in large saucepan and add water to cover by 1 to 2 inches. Season with salt and black pepper. Simmer until chicken is tender. Remove chicken and set aside. Prepare spaghetti, using chicken broth, according to package directions. Sauté onion and garlic in butter until tender. Add soups, tomatoes and cheese to vegetables and simmer until cheese is melted. Remove skin and bones from chicken and cut into bite-sized pieces. Drain spaghetti and add sauce and chicken, tossing to mix thoroughly. Yield: 10 servings.

White Chili with Salsa Verde

Combine water, lemon pepper and 1 teaspoon cumin in large saucepan. Bring to a boil. Add chicken and simmer, covered, for 30 minutes or until chicken is fork tender and juices run clear when pierced with fork tines. Remove chicken, cut into 1-inch chunks and return to saucepan. Sauté garlic in oil in skillet over medium heat for 30 seconds to 1 minute. Add garlic to chicken. Sauté onion in skillet until tender. Add onion, corn, chilies, 2 teaspoons cumin and lime juice to chicken. Bring chicken mixture to a boil. Add beans and cook until thoroughly heated; do not boil or stir excessively. If too thick, add small amount of chicken broth. To serve, place 1 tablespoon chips and cheese in individual soup bowls, then ladle hot soup over chips and cheese. Spoon green salsa on soup. Yield: 6 servings.

Note: Chili may be prepared several hours in advance, then reheated in the oven at 400° for 30 minutes just before serving.

2½ cups water
1 teaspoon lemon pepper
1 tablespoon cumin or to taste, divided
4 chicken breast halves, skin removed
4 cloves garlic, minced
1 teaspoon olive or canola oil
1 cup chopped white onion
2 9-ounce packages frozen shoepeg white corn, thawed, or 2 12-ounce cans shoepeg white corn, drained
2 4-ounce cans diced green chilies, undrained
1½ tablespoons lime juice
2 15-ounce cans great northern white beans, undrained
Crushed tortilla chips
1 cup (4 ounces) shredded low-fat Monterey Jack cheese
Green salsa

Yogurt Marinated Chicken

1 cup yogurt
  Juice of 1 large
  lime or lemon
4 scallions with tops,
  chopped
4 cloves garlic,
  minced
4 fresh jalapeño
  peppers, seeded and
  minced
1 bunch cilantro,
  chopped
1 teaspoon salt
1 teaspoon white
  pepper
2 teaspoons cumin
2 teaspoons chili
  powder
8 chicken breast
  halves, skin
  removed, boned and
  cut in halves

Combine yogurt, lime or lemon juice, scallions, garlic, jalapeño peppers, cilantro, salt, white pepper, cumin and chili powder in blender container. Process until smooth. Place chicken in baking dish. Pour yogurt mixture over chicken, turning to coat chicken pieces. Chill, covered, for 12 to 24 hours, turning pieces occasionally. Let chicken stand at room temperature before cooking. Drain chicken, reserving marinade. Grill about 4 to 6 inches above very hot coals, basting occasionally, for 5 to 8 minutes on each side or until done. Yield: 8 servings.

Baked Curry Chicken

½ cup butter, melted,
  divided
5 or 6 chicken thighs
½ cup honey
1 teaspoon salt
  (optional)
1 teaspoon curry
  powder

Pour ¼ cup butter into 8x8x2-inch baking pan. Place chicken in pan, turning to coat with butter. Combine ¼ cup butter, honey, salt and curry powder. Pour mixture over chicken, coating each piece. Bake at 375° for 45 minutes to 1 hour. Yield: 2 or 3 servings.

Chicken Margarita

**3 tablespoons olive
    oil, divided
    Juice of 3 limes
10 cloves garlic,
    minced
1 tablespoon chili
    powder
1 tablespoon cumin
3 to 3½ pounds
    chicken, cut up and
    skin removed
½ cup water
1 bunch cilantro for
    garnish**

Combine 1 tablespoon oil, lime juice, garlic, chili powder and cumin. Place chicken in marinade for 20 minutes. Remove chicken from marinade and sauté in 2 tablespoons oil in heavy skillet, turning to brown on all sides. Add marinade and water to chicken. Simmer, covered, for about 25 minutes or until chicken is thoroughly cooked. Transfer chicken to platter. Cook sauce over high heat until thickened and pour over chicken. Garnish with cilantro leaves. Serve with rice. Yield: 4 servings.

Spicy Chicken Skillet

**4 or 5 chicken breast
    halves
    Salt and black
    pepper to taste
    Paprika to taste
    Garlic powder to
    taste
    Vegetable oil
1 onion, diced
2 green bell peppers,
    diced
1½ cups instant rice
2 13-ounce cans
    chicken broth
1 tablespoon cumin
    seed**

Season chicken with salt, black pepper, paprika and garlic powder. Sauté chicken in oil in heavy oven-proof skillet, turning to brown on both sides. Remove chicken and set aside. Combine onion, green pepper and rice in skillet. Stir in broth and cumin. Add chicken to vegetables and rice mixture. Bring to a boil. Bake, covered, at 350° for 45 minutes. Yield: 4 or 5 servings.

Chicken Manicotti

Sauce

- ½ cup margarine
- ½ cup all-purpose flour
- 1½ teaspoons salt
  Dash of white pepper
- 1 cup milk
- 3½ cups chicken broth, divided
- ½ cup white wine

Melt butter in heavy saucepan. Blend in flour, salt, white pepper, milk and 1 cup broth. Cook over medium heat, stirring frequently, until sauce is thickened. Reserve ⅓ cup sauce for filling. Add 2½ cups broth and wine to remaining sauce. Bring to a boil, remove from heat and set aside.

Filling

- 1½ cups chopped cooked chicken
- 1¼ cups (5 ounces) grated Swiss cheese
- ⅓ cup reserved sauce
- ¼ cup white wine
- 1 egg, beaten
- 1 tablespoon minced parsley
- 1 clove garlic, crushed
- 1 16-ounce package manicotti shells
- 3 tablespoons grated Parmesan cheese

Combine chicken, Swiss cheese, reserved sauce, wine, egg, parsley and garlic. Spoon mixture into uncooked manicotti shells. Pour small amount of sauce into 2-quart rectangular baking dish. Arrange manicotti in single layer at least 1 inch apart on sauce. Pour remaining sauce over manicotti. Bake, covered, at 350° for 45 minutes. Spoon sauce over manicotti, sprinkle with Parmesan cheese and continue baking for 10 to 15 minutes on top oven rack to brown slightly. Yield: 4 servings.

Chicken Tetrazzini

Cook chicken in water until tender. Drain, reserving broth. Remove skin from chicken, bone and cut into bite-sized pieces. Sauté green pepper, celery and onion in butter in large saucepan until vegetables are tender. Add 1 cup reserved broth, soup, milk and flour to vegetables. Prepare spaghetti according to package directions, using reserved broth for cooking liquid. Drain well. Add chicken, spaghetti, cheese, salt and black pepper to sauce, mixing thoroughly. Spread spaghetti mixture in 13x9x2-inch baking dish. Bake at 350° for 30 minutes. Let stand for 10 to 15 minutes before serving. Yield: 8 to 10 servings.

10 chicken thighs
2 quarts water
½ cup chopped green pepper
1 cup chopped celery
½ cup chopped onion
¼ cup butter or margarine
1 10¾-ounce can cream of mushroom soup, undiluted
1 cup milk
3 tablespoons all-purpose flour
1 10-ounce package spaghetti
1 16-ounce package pasteurized process cheese spread, cubed
Salt and black pepper to taste

Swiss and Crab Pie

1 9-inch or 10-inch
   baked pastry shell
1 cup (4 ounces)
   shredded natural
   Swiss cheese
1 6½-ounce can crab
   meat, drained and
   flaked
2 green onions, sliced
3 eggs, beaten
1 cup half and half
¼ to ½ teaspoon
   grated lemon peel
¼ teaspoon dry
   mustard
   Dash of ground
   mace
¼ cup sliced almonds

In order listed, layer ingredients in pastry shell: cheese, crab meat and onion. Combine eggs, half and half, lemon peel, mustard and mace, mixing thoroughly. Pour egg liquid over onion layer. Sprinkle with almonds. Bake at 325° for 40 to 45 minutes or until knife tip inserted near center comes out clean. Let stand for 10 minutes before serving. Yield: 6 servings.

Bacalow

(Spanish Fish Casserole)

3 pounds dried cod
   Cold water
1 onion, chopped
2 tomatoes, chopped
½ cup chopped green
   olives
½ cup olive oil
2 2-ounce jars
   pimiento, drained
6 potatoes, peeled,
   cooked and
   quartered

Place fish in large saucepan. Add cold water, bring to a boil, drain and rinse thoroughly. Repeat process. Sauté onion, tomatoes and olives in oil in large skillet over low heat for about 15 minutes. Add pimiento, potatoes and cod. Simmer, covered, for 30 minutes. Yield: 6 servings.

Red Snapper Veracruzano

Sauté onion and garlic in 2 tablespoons oil until onion is tender. Add
jalapeño peppers, tomato sauce, lime or
lemon juice, 1 teaspoon salt, sugar,
cinnamon, cloves and ⅛ teaspoon
black pepper. Bring to a boil, reduce
heat and simmer, uncovered, for 5
minutes. Keep warm. Combine flour, 1
teaspoon salt and ⅛ teaspoon pepper.
Dredge fish in seasoned flour. Sauté
fish in ¼ cup oil in skillet over medium
heat for 4 minutes each side or until
golden brown, turning carefully.
Sprinkle olives on fish, spoon sauce
over fish and garnish with parsley.
Yield: 5 or 6 servings.

2 **medium-sized onions, chopped**
1 **clove garlic, chopped**
6 **tablespoons olive oil, divided**
2 **jalapeño peppers, seeded and cut in strips**
1 **15-ounce can tomato sauce**
1 **tablespoon lime or lemon juice**
2 **teaspoons salt, divided**
½ **teaspoon sugar**
⅛ **teaspoon cinnamon**
⅛ **teaspoon ground cloves**
¼ **teaspoon black pepper, divided**
¼ **cup all-purpose flour**
2 **pounds red snapper filets, cut in small pieces**
¼ **cup sliced pimiento-stuffed green olives Parsley sprigs for garnish**

Spetsae Baked Fish

¼ cup fresh lemon juice

1¼ teaspoons salt, divided

¼ teaspoon freshly ground white pepper

3 pounds sea bass, red snapper, cod or other firm fish fillets

1 bunch green onions with tops, chopped

2 stalks celery, minced

2 cloves garlic, minced

3 tablespoons olive oil

½ cup dry white wine

4 medium tomatoes, peeled and chopped

4 sprigs parsley, chopped

5 mint leaves, minced

2 medium tomatoes, sliced

¼ cup fine dry breadcrumbs

3 tablespoons butter, melted

Combine lemon juice, 1 teaspoon salt and white pepper. Marinate fish in lemon liquid in 13x9x2-inch baking dish in refrigerator for 1 hour. Sauté onion, celery and garlic in oil in large skillet over medium heat for 3 minutes. Stir in wine, chopped tomatoes, parsley, mint and ¼ teaspoon salt. Simmer, uncovered, over medium heat, stirring occasionally, for 20 minutes or until thickened. Let stand until slightly cool. Pour sauce over fish in baking dish. Arrange tomato slices on fish, sprinkle with breadcrumbs and drizzle with butter. Bake at 350° for 20 minutes or until fish flakes easily when probed with fork tines. Yield: 6 to 8 servings.

Sauté shrimp and onion in butter in skillet over medium heat until shrimp is pink. Stir in water and rice. Cook, covered, for 5 minutes. Blend flour and sour cream together. Add to rice and shrimp and heat thoroughly. Garnish with chives or sliced green onion tops. Yield: 4 servings.

Shrimp Elegante

1 pound shrimp, peeled and deveined
3 green onions, sliced
½ cup butter
2½ cups water
2⅓ cups instant rice
2 tablespoons all-purpose flour
2 cups sour cream
Chives or sliced green onion tops

Cook garlic in margarine in skillet over low heat for about 10 minutes. Discard garlic. Blend flour and broth mix into margarine. Combine milk and water. Add to flour mixture and cook over medium heat until thickened and smooth. Add cheese and stir until melted. Add oregano and cook for 10 minutes. Stir in parsley. Prepare spaghetti according to package directions and drain. Pour sauce over hot spaghetti and top with warm shrimp. Yield: 6 servings.

Shrimp Sauce for Spaghetti

1 large clove garlic, slashed
⅓ cup margarine
⅓ cup all-purpose flour
1 envelope instant chicken broth mix
1 14½-ounce can evaporated skim milk
1 cup water
¾ cup (3 ounces) grated Romano cheese
1 teaspoon oregano
½ cup chopped parsley
1 12-ounce package spaghetti
2 pounds cooked shrimp, peeled and deveined

Shrimp Creole

1 **bunch cilantro,
chopped**
3 **green bell peppers,
chopped**
2 **bunches celery,
chopped**
6 **medium-sized
onions, chopped**
1 **cup peanut oil**
1 **8-ounce can tomato
puree**
3 **46-ounce cans
vegetable cocktail
juice**
1 **10¾-ounce can beef
broth**
4 **cloves garlic,
crushed
Salt to taste**
½ **teaspoon black
pepper**
2 **tablespoons
paprika**
1 **teaspoon thyme**
1 **large bay leaf
Hot pepper sauce to
taste**
5 **pounds shrimp,
cooked, peeled and
deveined**
4 **teaspoons
cornstarch**

Sauté cilantro, green pepper, celery and onion in oil in heavy stockpot until onion is translucent. Add tomato puree, juice, broth, garlic, salt, black pepper, paprika, thyme, bay leaf and hot pepper sauce. Simmer for 30 minutes. Add shrimp and cornstarch, cooking until slightly thickened. Remove bay leaf. Serve over rice. Yield: 12 to 16 servings.

Combine margarine, crab boil, black pepper, mustard, thyme, basil, chili powder and hot pepper sauce in large oven-proof saucepan. Simmer for 5 minutes, stirring frequently. Add shrimp. Bake at 375° for 20 to 25 minutes. Serve with saffron rice. Yield: 3 or 4 servings.

Press spinach to remove excess moisture. Spread spinach in greased 2½-quart casserole. Sprinkle onion, tuna and eggs on spinach. Combine soup and sour cream. Pour soup mixture over eggs. Season with salt and black pepper. Combine butter and breadcrumbs and sprinkle on soup layer. Bake at 350° for 30 to 35 minutes or until golden brown and bubbly. Yield: 4 to 6 servings.

Cajun Barbecued Shrimp

1½ cups margarine
3 to 5 tablespoons crab boil or to taste
1 tablespoon black pepper
2 tablespoons Dijon mustard
1 tablespoon thyme
1 tablespoon basil
1½ teaspoons chili powder
   Hot pepper sauce to taste
1½ pounds fresh shrimp, peeled and deveined

Tuna Florentine

2 10-ounce packages frozen chopped spinach, thawed
2 tablespoons minced onion flakes
1 6¼-ounce can tuna, drained
6 hard-cooked eggs, sliced
2 10¾-ounce cans cream of mushroom soup, undiluted
1 cup sour cream
   Salt and black pepper to taste
¼ cup melted butter
2 cups soft breadcrumbs

Gram's Gumbo

4 to 6 slices bacon
16 small okra pods
1 large onion, chopped
1 small green bell pepper, chopped
1 clove garlic, sliced
2½ tablespoons all-purpose flour
3 cups chicken broth or consommé
1 stalk celery, chopped
½ cup canned tomatoes, chopped
1 bay leaf
1 teaspoon Worcestershire sauce
Salt and black pepper to taste
½ teaspoon thyme
2 cups cooked shrimp
1 cup crab meat or white flaked tuna
1 tablespoon file powder

Sauté bacon in large heavy skillet for 2 minutes. Remove from skillet, cut into small pieces and set aside. Sauté okra, onion and green pepper in bacon drippings over low heat for about 5 minutes. Add garlic and flour, stirring and cooking until flour is browned. Add broth, celery, tomatoes, bay leaf, Worcestershire sauce, salt, black pepper and thyme. Simmer, covered, for 1 hour. Stir in shrimp and crab. Cook for 2 minutes, then add file powder. Serve over rice. Yield: 4 servings.

Jalapeño Quiche

1 4-ounce can jalapeño peppers, chopped and drained
8 cups (32 ounces) grated Cheddar cheese
1 dozen eggs

Place peppers in casserole. Add cheese. Beat eggs until frothy and pour over cheese. Bake at 350° for 45 minutes. Let stand for 10 minutes before cutting into squares to serve. Yield: 12 servings.

RIPE FOR THE HARVEST

I tell you, open your eyes
and look at the fields!
They are ripe for harvest.
JOHN 4: 35

VEGETABLES

Falafel

Filling

¼ **cup fine bulgar**
Hot water
2 **cups cooked**
garbanzo beans,
mashed
2 **cloves garlic,**
minced
3 **tablespoons**
breadcrumbs
1 **egg, beaten**
½ **teaspoon salt**
¼ **teaspoon black**
pepper
½ **teaspoon cumin**
¼ **teaspoon coriander**
1 **tablespoon minced**
parsley
⅛ **teaspoon cayenne**
pepper
All-purpose flour
Vegetable oil
4 **to 5 pita bread**
rounds
Tahini

Soak bulgar in hot water for 20 minutes. Drain. Combine bulgar, beans, garlic, breadcrumbs, egg, salt, black pepper, cumin, coriander, parsley and cayenne pepper, mixing thoroughly. Chill for 1 hour. Shape mixture into 16 balls, dredge in flour and deep fry in oil until golden brown. Drain on paper towel. Cut a slit in pita, fill with falafel, tahini and relish. Yield: 4 to 5 servings.

Relish

2 **ripe tomatoes,**
peeled and minced
½ **cup chopped**
parsley
1 **green bell pepper,**
minced
1 **cucumber, peeled**
and minced
Salt and black
pepper to taste
Cayenne pepper to
taste

Combine tomatoes, parsley, green pepper, cucumber, salt, black pepper and cayenne pepper, mixing thoroughly. Serve with falafel.

Baked Pork and Beans

Sauté bacon until crisp. Combine beans, ketchup, liquid smoke, brown sugar and onion, mixing thoroughly. Add bacon and drippings. Pour into 2½-quart casserole. Bake at 350° for 1 hour. Yield: 10 servings.

4 slices bacon, diced
3 16-ounce cans pork and beans
1 cup ketchup
2 tablespoons liquid smoke
¾ cup firmly-packed brown sugar
1 medium-sized onion, thinly sliced

Green Bean Casserole

Place beans in 12x8x2-inch baking dish. Layer potatoes on beans. Melt margarine in small saucepan. Stir in flour, add milk and cook until sauce is thickened. Stir in sour cream, salt and white pepper. Pour sauce over potatoes. Sprinkle with cheese. Bake at 350° for 45 minutes to 1 hour. Yield: 8 servings.

2 16-ounce cans whole green beans, drained
8 to 10 small new potatoes, cooked and sliced
½ cup margarine
1 tablespoon all-purpose flour
1 cup milk
1 cup sour cream
Salt and white pepper to taste
1 cup (4 ounces) grated Cheddar cheese

Sweet and Sour Green Beans

3 slices bacon
1 16-ounce can green
    beans, drained
¼ cup vinegar
¼ cup sugar

Sauté bacon in saucepan until crisp. Remove bacon, drain and crumble. Combine beans, vinegar and sugar in saucepan. Simmer for 15 minutes. Sprinkle bacon on bean mixture. Yield: 3 servings.

Fettuchini with Three Cheese Sauce

¼ cup margarine
½ cup half and half
½ cup shredded
    Gruyère cheese
¼ cup grated
    Parmesan cheese
½ teaspoon salt
⅛ teaspoon ground
    pepper
    Minced garlic to
    taste
1 8-ounce package
    fettuchini,
    uncooked
2 tablespoons olive
    oil
½ cup mozzarella
    cheese
1 tablespoon parsley

Heat margarine and half and half in 2-quart saucepan over low heat until margarine is melted. Add Gruyère and Parmesan cheeses, salt, pepper and garlic. Stir for 5 minutes. Cook fettuchini according to package directions, adding olive oil to boiling water. Drain. Add fettuchini to sauce. Add mozzarella and toss. Sprinkle with parsley and serve.

Best Broccoli Casserole

Prepare broccoli according to package directions. Drain and place in buttered 2-quart shallow casserole. Combine mayonnaise, soup, eggs and onion in blender container. Process until smooth. Pour sauce over broccoli and sprinkle with cheese and breadcrumbs. Bake at 350° for about 45 minutes or until bubbly. Yield: 5 or 6 servings.

2 10-ounce packages frozen chopped broccoli
½ cup mayonnaise
1 10¾-ounce can Cheddar cheese soup, undiluted
2 eggs
¼ cup chopped onion
½ cup (2 ounces) grated cheese (optional)
½ cup breadcrumbs

Sesame Broccoli

Combine oil, vinegar, soy sauce and sugar in small saucepan. Toast sesame seed at 450° until lightly browned. Pour sauce over broccoli and sprinkle with sesame seed just before serving. Yield: 4 or 5 servings.

3 tablespoons vegetable oil
3 tablespoons vinegar
3 tablespoons soy sauce
¼ cup sugar
¼ cup sesame seed
1 pound fresh broccoli, cooked and drained

Brussels Sprouts with Ham

1 pound Brussels
   sprouts
2 cups chicken broth
1 small onion, thinly
   sliced
2 tablespoons
   margarine
¼ cup minced smoked
   ham
2 tablespoons grated
   Parmesan cheese

Combine Brussels sprouts and broth in saucepan. Bring to a boil, reduce heat and simmer, covered, for 10 minutes or until tender. Drain and set aside. Sauté onion in margarine in skillet over medium heat, stirring frequently, until onion is tender. Add Brussels sprouts and ham. Simmer, covered, for 2 minutes or until thoroughly heated. Sprinkle with cheese. Yield: 4 servings.

French Cabbage

1 medium head
   cabbage, quartered
   Water
   Salt
¾ cup chopped celery
1½ green bell peppers,
   chopped
3 or 4 cloves garlic,
   minced
1 to 2 tablespoons
   butter or margarine
1 cup half and half
1 cup (4 ounces)
   shredded Cheddar
   cheese
   Salt and black
   pepper to taste
⅓ cup buttered
   breadcrumbs

Cook cabbage in small amount of salted water for 5 to 8 minutes or until tender. Drain. Chop cabbage to shredded consistency. Sauté celery, green pepper and garlic in butter in saucepan, covered, over low heat until vegetables are tender. Add vegetables to cabbage. Stir half and half, cheese, salt and black pepper into vegetables, mixing thoroughly. Pour cabbage mixture into buttered 1½-quart casserole. Sprinkle with breadcrumbs. Bake at 300° for 30 minutes. Yield: 6 to 8 servings.

Stuffed Cabbage Rolls

Combine rices and broth in saucepan. Cook, covered, for 30 minutes. Combine spaghetti sauce, brown sugar and Worcestershire sauce in saucepan. Simmer while preparing other ingredients. Cook cabbage leaves in water for 15 minutes, drain, rinse in cold water and set aside. Sauté sausage, turkey, onion, garlic, salt, black pepper, tarragon and grated cabbage in oil in large skillet, cooking for 10 to 15 minutes or until meat is nearly done. Add cooked rice to meat mixture. Place ½ cup meat mixture on each cabbage leaf, fold sides and roll up to enclose. Pour thin layer of spaghetti sauce mixture in 12x8x2-inch baking pan. Place rolls, seam side down, on sauce. Spoon remaining sauce over rolls. Bake, covered, at 300° for 45 minutes. Yield: 6 to 8 servings.

¾ cup uncooked regular rice
¼ cup uncooked wild rice
2½ cups chicken broth
1 30-ounce can spaghetti sauce
2 tablespoons brown sugar
2 teaspoons Worcestershire sauce
8 to 10 cabbage leaves
Water
1 pound turkey breakfast sausage
1 pound ground turkey
1 onion, chopped
4 cloves garlic, minced
Salt and black pepper to taste
½ teaspoon dried tarragon
1 cup grated cabbage
2 tablespoons canola oil

Eggplant Parmesan

Eggplant
- **1 large eggplant, cut in ¼-inch slices**
- **Salt and black pepper to taste**
- **2 eggs, beaten**
- **1½ cups cracker crumbs**
- **Vegetable oil**
- **2 cups (8 ounces) shredded mozzarella cheese**
- **6 tablespoons (3 ounces) grated Parmesan cheese**

Season eggplant slices with salt and black pepper and place in bowl. Let stand for 30 minutes, rinse and blot dry with paper towel. Dip slices in egg, coat with crumbs and sauté in oil until golden brown. Drain on paper towel. Place ½ of slices in lightly-greased 12x8x2-inch baking dish. Spoon ½ of Quick Italian Sauce over slices and sprinkle with ½ of mozzarella and Parmesan cheeses. Repeat layers. Bake at 350° for 20 to 25 minutes or until thoroughly heated. Yield: 6 servings.

Quick Italian Sauce
- **½ cup chopped onion**
- **1 clove garlic, minced**
- **1 tablespoon vegetable oil**
- **1 12-ounce can tomato paste**
- **1 10½-ounce can tomato soup, undiluted**
- **1¼ cups water**
- **1½ teaspoons dried oregano**
- **½ teaspoon ground basil**

Sauté onion and garlic in oil until tender. Add tomato paste and soup, water, oregano and basil. Bring to a boil, reduce heat and simmer for 15 minutes, stirring occasionally.

Marinated Carrots

Cook carrots in small amount of water until just tender. Drain and set aside to cool. Combine soup, oil, vinegar, sugar, salt and black pepper in blender container. Process until smooth. Pour marinade over carrots. Add onion, bell pepper and green beans. Store in glass jar or dish in refrigerator for up to 2 weeks. After vegetables are consumed, excess marinade may be used for salad dressing. Yield: 10 to 12 servings.

2 pounds carrots, sliced
Water
1 10½-ounce can tomato soup, undiluted
1 cup canola oil
¾ cup cider vinegar
1 cup sugar
1 teaspoon salt
½ teaspoon black pepper
1 medium-sized onion, chopped
1 green bell pepper, chopped
1 16-ounce can green beans, drained

Mexican Hominy

Combine onion, bacon drippings, sugar and tomatoes, in saucepan. Bring to a boil and cook until onion is tender. Add hominy and simmer until done. Stir in cheese and cook until melted. Season with chili powder just before serving. Yield: 4 servings.

1 large onion, minced
Bacon drippings to taste
½ teaspoon sugar
1 10-ounce can tomatoes with chilies
1 16-ounce can hominy, drained
Pasteurized process cheese spread, cubed, to taste
Chili powder to taste

Mexican Mushrooms

2 medium tomatoes, minced
1 tablespoon vegetable oil
½ onion, minced
2 or 3 jalapeño peppers, minced
½ pound fresh mushrooms or 1 8-ounce can, drained

Sauté tomatoes in oil for 5 minutes. Add onion, jalapeño peppers and mushrooms. Simmer for 10 minutes. Serve as accompaniment or place in tortilla with dollop of sour cream and top with slice of avocado. Yield: 4 to 6 servings.

Baked Potato Wedges

½ cup all-purpose flour
1 teaspoon salt
¾ teaspoon black pepper
½ teaspoon chili powder
½ teaspoon garlic salt
½ teaspoon onion salt
½ cup (2 ounces) grated Parmesan cheese
8 or 9 medium potatoes, cut in wedges
Cold water
½ cup butter

Combine flour, salt, black pepper, chili powder, garlic salt, onion salt and Parmesan cheese. Soak potatoes in cold water, drain and dredge in seasoned flour. Melt butter in 13x9x2-inch baking pan. Place potatoes on melted butter. Bake at 375° for 30 to 40 minutes. Yield: 5 or 6 servings.

Twice Baked Potatoes

Combine potatoes, margarine, milk, cheese, bacon, onion, chives and salt. Pour mixture into buttered 2-quart casserole. Bake at 350° for 20 to 30 minutes. Serve with dollop of sour cream and sprinkle with chives. Yield: 4 or 5 servings.

3 large potatoes, baked, diced and cooled
¼ cup melted margarine
2 tablespoons milk
1 cup (4 ounces) shredded Cheddar cheese
4 slices bacon, cooked, drained and crumbled
1 tablespoon onion flakes
1 tablespoon chopped chives
½ teaspoon salt
Sour cream
Chopped chives

Red Potato Casserole

Combine hot water and soup mix. Stir in margarine, parsley and black pepper. Pour liquid into buttered 2-quart casserole. Add potatoes. Bake, covered, at 350° for 1½ hours; remove cover and continue baking for 30 minutes. Yield: 4 servings.

1 cup hot water
1 envelope onion soup mix
¼ cup margarine, melted
½ teaspoon parsley
¼ teaspoon black pepper
8 medium-sized red potatoes, peeled and cut in ½-inch cubes

Cheese Potato Casserole

1 32-ounce package frozen grated hash brown potatoes, thawed
2 10¾-ounce cans cream of potato soup, undiluted
1 cup sour cream
2 cups (8 ounces) grated Cheddar cheese
¼ cup (1 ounce) grated Parmesan cheese

Combine potatoes, soup, sour cream and Cheddar cheese. Spread mixture in buttered 13x9x2-inch baking pan. Sprinkle Parmesan cheese on potato mixture. Bake at 300° for 1½ hours. Yield: 12 to 16 servings.

Scrivener's Spinach Soufflé

1 small onion, chopped
⅓ cup butter
½ cup all-purpose flour
½ teaspoon salt
2 cups milk
2 eggs, lightly beaten
3 cups cooked spinach
1 cup (4 ounces) grated pasteurized process cheese spread

Sauté onion in butter until tender. Stir in flour, salt and milk. Cook to form white sauce, remove from heat and set aside to cool. Add eggs to cooled sauce. Stir in spinach and cheese, mixing thoroughly. Pour spinach mixture into buttered 2-quart casserole. Bake at 350° until firm and wooden pick inserted near center comes out clean. Yield: 5 or 6 servings.

Okra Casserole

Combine flour and cornmeal. Dredge okra in flour mixture. Sauté okra, onion and green pepper in oil until tender. Add corn and tomatoes. Simmer for 5 minutes. Stir in salt, black pepper, oregano and garlic powder, mixing thoroughly. Layer vegetables, cheeses and breadcrumbs in buttered 3-quart casserole, ending with cheese and crumb layers. Bake at 350° for 30 minutes or until cheese is bubbly. Yield: 8 to 10 servings.

¼ cup all-purpose flour
¼ cup cornmeal
3 pounds okra, cut in 1-inch pieces
1 large onion, chopped
1 large green bell pepper, chopped
¼ cup olive oil
2 ears corn, cut from cob, or 1 8-ounce can corn, drained
3 large tomatoes, chopped
Salt and black pepper to taste
½ teaspoon oregano
½ teaspoon garlic powder
½ cup (2 ounces) grated mozzarella cheese
1 cup (4 ounces) grated longhorn cheese
Grated Parmesan cheese
½ cup breadcrumbs

Squash Casserole

½ cup melted butter
   or margarine
1 8-ounce package
   herb seasoned
   stuffing mix
2 pounds yellow
   squash, cooked and
   drained
2 small carrots,
   grated
2 small onions,
   chopped
1 10¾-ounce can
   cream of chicken
   soup, undiluted
1 cup sour cream

Combine butter and stuffing mix. Pour ½ of mixture in 12x8x2-inch baking dish. Combine squash, carrots, onion, soup and sour cream. Spread vegetable mixture on crumbs and sprinkle with remaining crumbs. Bake at 350° for at least 30 minutes. Yield: 6 to 8 servings.

Squash Winner's Casserole

3 medium-sized
   yellow squash,
   sliced
Water
Salt
⅓ cup (5 ounces)
   shredded Cheddar
   cheese
1 medium-sized white
   onion, chopped
1 egg, beaten
½ teaspoon salt
¼ teaspoon black
   pepper
¼ cup margarine,
   divided
½ cup bread or
   cracker crumbs

Cook squash in small amount of salted water until tender. Drain well. Combine squash, cheese, onion, egg, salt, black pepper, 2 tablespoons margarine and ¼ cup crumbs. Spread mixture in buttered 1½-quart casserole. Dot with 2 tablespoons margarine and ¼ cup crumbs. Bake at 375° for 10 minutes. Yield: 4 to 6 servings.

Zucchini Patties

Combine zucchini, onion, parsley, sage, bouillon granules and small amount of water in saucepan. Simmer, covered, until tender. Let stand until cool. Add egg and cracker crumbs to zucchini mixture. Drop tablespoonfuls of mixture into hot oil, turning to brown on both sides. Yield: 6 servings.

- 2 pounds grated zucchini
- ¼ cup chopped onion
- 1 teaspoon parsley
- ⅛ teaspoon sage
- 1 teaspoon chicken bouillon granules
- Water
- 1 egg, beaten
- 6 saltines, crushed
- ¼ cup olive oil

Mushroom Stuffed Tomatoes

Cut stem end from tomatoes, scoop out pulp and invert to drain. Finely chop 1 cup tomato pulp and set aside. Sauté mushrooms in butter until tender. Combine sour cream and egg yolks. Add egg mixture, tomato pulp, breadcrumbs, salt, black pepper, thyme and hot pepper sauce to mushrooms, mixing well. Simmer until thickened. Place tomato shells in buttered 8x8x2-inch baking dish. Spoon mushroom mixture into shells and sprinkle with cheese. Bake at 375° for 25 minutes. Yield: 6 servings.

Variation: 1 cup grated cheese may be added to mushroom mixture after it is cooked and thickened.

- 6 medium tomatoes
- 2 cups fresh mushrooms, sliced
- 2 tablespoons butter
- ½ cup sour cream
- 2 egg yolks, beaten
- ¼ cup Italian seasoned breadcrumbs
- ½ teaspoon salt
- Black pepper to taste
- ⅛ teaspoon thyme
- 4 drops hot pepper sauce
- ½ cup (2 ounces) grated cheese

Tomato Pie

3 large tomatoes, sliced
1 9-inch baked deep-dish pastry shell
8 green onions, chopped
12 slices bacon, cooked, drained and crumbled
1½ cups (6 ounces) grated Cheddar cheese
1½ cups mayonnaise

Arrange tomato slices in pastry shell. Sprinkle onion and bacon on tomatoes. Combine cheese and mayonnaise. Spread mixture evenly on onion and bacon layer. Bake at 350° for 30 minutes. Yield: 6 to 8 servings.

Ratatouille

1 eggplant, peeled and cubed
Salt
2 tablespoons olive oil
2 tablespoons margarine
1 large onion, chopped
2 green bell peppers, chopped
4 zucchini, cubed
4 to 6 tomatoes, cubed
2 cloves garlic, chopped
2 tablespoons dried parsley
1 teaspoon oregano
½ cup (2 ounces) grated Parmesan cheese
Freshly ground black pepper

Sprinkle eggplant with salt and let stand for 20 to 30 minutes. Sauté eggplant in oil and margarine in large skillet until tender. Remove eggplant from skillet. Adding more oil if necessary, sauté onion, green pepper, zucchini, tomatoes and garlic, cooking until tender. Combine eggplant, vegetable mixture, parsley, oregano and cheese. Season with salt and black pepper. Pour vegetable mixture into buttered 13x9x2-inch baking dish. Bake at 300° for 15 minutes. Yield: 8 to 12 servings.

Vegetable Casserole

Combine zucchini, eggplant, green pepper and tomatoes. Sauté onion, garlic and parsley in oil in 6-quart Dutch oven until transparent but not browned. Stir in vegetables, tomato paste, sugar, salt, red pepper flakes, basil, marjoram and wine, tossing gently to mix. Cook, covered, over medium heat for about 30 minutes or just until vegetables are tender, stirring occasionally. Sprinkle cheese on individual servings. Yield: 6 to 8 servings.

1 **pound zucchini, cut in ¼-inch slices**
1 **pound eggplant, peeled and cut in 1-inch cubes**
1 **pound green bell peppers, cut in ¼-inch strips**
1 **16-ounce can whole tomatoes, undrained**
¼ **cup chopped red onion**
1 **large clove garlic, minced**
1 **tablespoon chopped parsley**
3 **tablespoons olive oil**
3 **tablespoons tomato paste**
½ **teaspoon sugar**
2 **teaspoons salt Pinch of red pepper flakes**
1½ **teaspoons dried basil**
1½ **teaspoons dried marjoram**
¼ **cup dry white wine**

Green Rice

¾ **cup minced**
 scallions
 4 **tablespoons butter,**
 divided
 ½ **cup minced parsley**
1½ **cups chopped**
 spinach
 2 **cups uncooked long**
 grain white rice
 ½ **teaspoon salt**
 1 **teaspoon black**
 pepper
 2 **cups hot chicken**
 broth
 2 **tablespoons**
 chopped basil
 ¼ **cup (1 ounce)**
 grated Parmesan
 cheese

Sauté scallions in 3 tablespoons butter for 2 minutes or until soft. Stir in parsley and spinach. Cook until spinach is wilted. Add rice, salt and black pepper, mixing thoroughly. Add broth and stir until creamy. Cook for 15 to 20 minutes. Remove from heat and stir in basil, 1 tablespoon butter and cheese. Yield: 4 to 6 servings.

Rice Pilaf

 1 **cup uncooked**
 regular rice
 1 **10½-ounce can beef**
 broth
 1 **10¾-ounce can**
 onion soup
 ½ **cup margarine,**
 cubed
 2 **4-ounce cans**
 mushrooms,
 drained

Combine rice, broth, soup, margarine and mushrooms. Pour mixture into buttered 2-quart casserole. Bake, covered, at 350° for 1 hour or until firm. Yield: 4 servings.

SWEET SAVOR

Honey from the comb
is sweet to your taste.

Know also
that wisdom
is sweet to the soul.
PROVERBS 24: 13,14

DESSERTS

Angel Sweets

1 6-ounce package
  semi-sweet
  chocolate chips
2 tablespoons
  margarine
1 egg, beaten
1 cup powdered sugar
2 cups miniature
  marshmallows
1 cup finely chopped
  nuts
1 cup grated coconut

Combine chocolate chips and margarine in top of double boiler. Cook over simmering water until chips are melted. Remove from heat. Blend in egg and powdered sugar. Add marshmallows and nuts, mixing thoroughly. Shape mixture into 1-inch balls and roll in coconut. Chill until firm and store in cool place. Yield: 6 dozen.

Million Dollar Fudge

3 3¾-ounce chocolate
  candy bars, broken
  into pieces
1 12-ounce package
  chocolate chips
1 7-ounce jar
  marshmallow
  creme
1 tablespoon
  margarine
1 teaspoon vanilla
4½ cups sugar
1 14½-ounce can
  evaporated milk
1½ cups chopped
  pecans

Combine candy bar pieces, chocolate chips, marshmallow creme, margarine and vanilla. Combine sugar and milk in large saucepan. Bring to a boil and cook for 6 minutes. Pour sugar mixture over candy mixture, blending until smooth and creamy. Stir in pecans. Pour mixture into buttered pans or shallow dishes. Let stand for 4 to 6 hours or until completely cooled. Yield: 3 pounds.

Divinity

Combine syrup and water in saucepan. Add sugar and stir to dissolve. Cook over high heat until syrup will spin a thread. Add ½ of syrup to egg white, beating well. Add remaining syrup, vanilla and pecans, beating well. Drop by teaspoonfuls on buttered surface. Yield: 1 pound.

- ½ **cup light corn syrup**
- ½ **cup water**
- 2¼ **cups sugar**
- 1 **egg white, well beaten**
- 1 **teaspoon vanilla**
- 2 **cups pecans**

English Toffee

Melt butter in large saucepan. Add almonds, sugar, syrup and water, stirring until sugar is dissolved. Cook, stirring frequently, to 290° on candy thermometer. Remove from heat. Stir in vanilla and pour onto baking sheet lined with aluminum foil. Sprinkle chocolate chips on hot toffee layer, spreading evenly as chocolate melts. Store pieces of toffee in air-tight plastic bags. Yield: 3 pounds.

- 2 **cups butter or 1 cup butter plus 1 cup margarine**
- 1½ **cups chopped raw almonds**
- 2 **cups sugar**
- 2 **tablespoons light corn syrup**
- ⅓ **cup water**
- 1 **teaspoon vanilla**
- 1 **12-ounce package milk chocolate chips**

Easy Pecan Logs

Combine marshmallow creme, powdered sugar and vanilla. Mixture will be dry. Shape into 4 logs and chill for 2 to 3 hours. Melt caramels in top of double boiler over moderately boiling water. Dip chilled logs, 1 at a time, into melted caramel and roll in pecans. Chill for 1½ to 2 hours before cutting into 2-inch slices for serving. Yield: 1⅔ pounds.

- 1 **7-ounce jar marshmallow creme**
- 1 **16-ounce package powdered sugar**
- 1 **teaspoon vanilla**
- 1 **14-ounce package vanilla caramels Coarsely chopped pecans**

195

Peanut Brittle

3 cups sugar
1 cup light corn
   syrup
1⅓ cups water
¾ pound raw Spanish
   peanuts
¼ cup butter
2½ teaspoons baking
   soda
2 teaspoons vanilla

Combine sugar, syrup and water in saucepan. Cook, stirring frequently, until sugar is dissolved. Cook, covered, for 5 minutes. Remove cover and cook until syrup reaches 275° on candy thermometer. Reduce heat and add peanuts and butter. Cook, stirring frequently, until peanuts are cooked and syrup is light golden brown. Combine baking soda and vanilla. Remove syrup from heat and add vanilla mixture. Mixture will fizz. Pour on foil-lined baking sheet and smooth to thickness of 1 peanut. Yield: 2 pounds.

Creamy Pecan Pralines

1 cup sugar
2 cups firmly-packed
   brown sugar
½ teaspoon baking
   soda
1 cup sour cream
¼ cup light corn
   syrup
¼ teaspoon salt
1 tablespoon butter
1 teaspoon vanilla
1½ to 2 cups chopped
   pecans, toasted

Combine sugars, baking soda, sour cream, corn syrup and salt in heavy saucepan. Cook, stirring frequently, over medium heat until sugar is dissolved. Cover until mixture begins to boil; remove cover and cook, without stirring, to soft ball stage or 234° on candy thermometer. Remove from heat and add butter and vanilla; do not stir. Let stand until lukewarm. Beat until creamy and thickened. Add nuts. Quickly drop by teaspoonfuls on buttered baking sheet, spreading into 2 to 3-inch patties. Wrap firm pralines in plastic wrap and store in tightly-covered container. Yield: 2 dozen.

Sugared Nuts

Place nuts on baking sheet. Bake at
300° for 15 minutes. Combine sugar,
cinnamon, salt and water in saucepan.
Bring to a boil and cook to soft ball
stage of 234° on candy thermometer.
Remove from heat and add vanilla.
Stir in nuts and mix until all are
coated. Pour nuts on buttered surface.
Let stand until cool, gently separating.
Yield: 1¼ pounds.

**4 cups walnut or
    pecan halves**
1 cup sugar
1 teaspoon cinnamon
1 teaspoon salt
½ cup water
1½ teaspoons vanilla

Caramelized Popcorn

Combine sugar, syrup and margarine
in saucepan. Bring to a boil and cook
for 5 minutes. Remove from heat. Add
cream of tartar, baking soda and salt.
Stir until ball forms. Pour over popcorn and nuts, mixing to distribute
evenly. Pour popcorn mixture into
baking pan prepared with non-stick
vegetable spray. Bake at 200° for 1
hour, stirring occasionally. Yield: 6
quarts.

**2 cups firmly-packed
    light brown sugar**
**½ cup light corn
    syrup**
**1 cup margarine
    Pinch of cream of
    tartar**
**½ teaspoon baking
    soda
    Dash of salt**
6 quarts popped corn
**1½ to 2 cups mixed
    nuts**

Butterscotch Goodie Bars

½ **cup vegetable oil**
2 **cups firmly-packed brown sugar**
2 **eggs, beaten**
1½ **cups all-purpose flour**
1 **teaspoon baking powder**
1 **teaspoon salt**
1 **teaspoon vanilla**
1 **6-ounce package butterscotch chips**
1½ **cups pecans**

Cream oil and sugar together until smooth. Add eggs, beating thoroughly. Combine flour, baking powder and salt. Add dry ingredients to creamed mixture. Add vanilla and butterscotch chips. Spread dough on well-greased and floured 15x10x1-inch baking sheet. Press pecans into dough surface. Bake at 350° for 25 minutes. Let cool before cutting into bars. Yield: 4 dozen.

Note: *Bars may be frozen.*

Caramel Pecan Dream Bars

1 **18½-ounce package yellow cake mix**
½ **cup margarine or butter, softened**
2 **eggs, divided**
1 **14-ounce can sweetened condensed milk**
1 **teaspoon vanilla**
½ **cup butter brickle baking chips**
1 **cup chopped pecans**

Combine cake mix, margarine and 1 egg. Using electric mixer at highest speed, beat mixture until crumb consistency. Press crumbs into greased 13x9x2-inch baking pan. Combine milk, 1 egg and vanilla, beating until well blended. Stir in chips and pecans. Pour mixture over crumb layer, spreading to cover evenly. Bake at 350° for 25 to 35 minutes; center may appear soft but will firm on cooling. Cool bars before cutting. Yield: 4 dozen.

Carrot Cookies

Cookies

- ¾ **cup vegetable shortening**
- ¾ **cup sugar**
- 1 **cup mashed cooked carrots**
- 1 **egg**
- 1 **teaspoon vanilla**
- 2 **cups sifted all-purpose flour**
- 2 **teaspoons baking powder**
- ¼ **teaspoon salt**

Cream shortening and sugar together until smooth. Add carrots, egg and vanilla. Combine flour, baking powder and salt. Add dry ingredients to carrot mixture, mixing thoroughly. Drop dough by teaspoonfuls on lightly greased baking sheets. Bake at 350° for 20 minutes. Spread frosting on warm cookies. Yield: 2½ to 3 dozen.

Frosting

- 2½ **tablespoons orange juice**
- 1½ **teaspoons butter, softened**
- 1½ **teaspoons grated orange peel**
  Powdered sugar

Combine juice, butter, orange peel and enough powdered sugar to form spreading consistency. Spread frosting on warm cookies.

Blonde Caramel Brownies

- ½ **cup vegetable shortening**
- 2 **cups firmly-packed brown sugar**
- 2 **teaspoons vanilla**
- 2 **eggs**
- 1 **cup all-purpose flour**
- 1 **teaspoon baking powder**
- 1 **teaspoon salt**
- 1 **cup chopped nuts**

Melt shortening in large saucepan. Add sugar and vanilla, mixing thoroughly. Let stand until cool. Add eggs, 1 at a time, beating well after each addition. Sift flour, baking powder and salt together. Add dry ingredients to egg mixture. Stir in nuts. Spread dough in lightly greased 13x9x2-inch baking pan. Bake at 325° for 30 minutes. Let cool before cutting into squares. Yield: 2 dozen.

Chocolate Caramel Brownies

1 16-ounce package
   caramels
⅔ cup evaporated
   milk, divided
1 18½-ounce package
   German chocolate
   cake mix
¾ cup melted butter
1 12-ounce package
   chocolate chips
1 cup chopped pecans

Combine caramels and ⅓ cup evaporated milk in large saucepan. Cook over low heat, stirring constantly, until caramels are melted. Combine cake mix, butter and ⅓ cup evaporated milk, stirring by hand to mix thoroughly. Pour ½ of batter into greased and floured 13x9x2-inch baking pan. Bake at 350° for 6 minutes. Sprinkle chocolate chips and pecans over partially baked batter and drizzle with caramel mixture. Pour remaining cake batter over caramel layer. Bake for 18 minutes. Cool before cutting into bars. Brownies may also be served warm with vanilla ice cream. Yield: 2 dozen.

Graham Cracker Brownies

2½ cups graham
   cracker crumbs
1 13-ounce can
   sweetened
   condensed milk
1 3-ounce package
   chopped nuts
1 6-ounce package
   chocolate chips

Combine crumbs, milk, nuts and chips, mixing thoroughly. Spread batter in greased and floured 8x8x2-inch baking pan. Bake at 350° for 30 minutes. Yield: 1¼ dozen.

White House Brownies

Combine margarine and chocolate in saucepan. Melt over low heat, stirring until smooth and blended. Sift flour, baking powder and salt together. Beat eggs and sugar together until light in color. Blend in chocolate mixture. Add dry ingredients, vanilla and nuts, mixing thoroughly. Spread batter in 18x12x2-inch baking pan prepared by buttering and dusting with cocoa. Bake at 350° for 30 to 35 minutes. Yield: 4½ dozen.

Note: Brownies may be frozen.

½ cup margarine
3 1-ounce squares semi-sweet chocolate
2 1-ounce squares unsweetened chocolate
⅔ cup cake flour
1 teaspoon baking powder
1 teaspoon salt
6 eggs
2 cups sugar
1 tablespoon vanilla
2 cups chopped nuts

White Chocolate Brownies

Sift flour, baking powder and salt together. Combine sugar, eggs and almond extract, beating thoroughly. Blend in butter and white chocolate. Gradually add dry ingredients. Pour batter into greased 9x9x2-inch baking dish. Sprinkle almonds on batter. Bake at 350° for 25 to 30 minutes. Cool before cutting into squares. Yield: 1¼ dozen.

1½ cups all-purpose flour
½ teaspoon baking powder
¼ teaspoon salt
⅔ cup sugar
2 eggs
1 teaspoon almond extract
⅓ cup butter, melted, at room temperature
3 6-ounce white chocolate candy bars, melted
⅓ cup sliced almonds

Chocolate Syrup Brownies

Brownies
- 1 cup sugar
- ½ cup margarine, softened
- 4 eggs
- 1 12-ounce can chocolate syrup
- 1 cup all-purpose flour
- ¼ teaspoon baking soda
- 1 teaspoon vanilla

Cream sugar and margarine together until smooth. Add eggs, 1 at a time, beating well after each addition. Add syrup, flour, baking soda and vanilla, mixing thoroughly. Spread batter in 15x10x1-inch baking sheet. Bake at 350° for 25 minutes. Cool before spreading with frosting and cutting into bars. Yield: 3 dozen.

Frosting
- 1½ cups sugar
- ⅓ cup milk or half and half
- ½ cup chocolate chips
- ½ cup margarine
- 1 teaspoon vanilla

Combine sugar and milk in saucepan. Bring to a boil, cook for 1 minute and remove from heat. Stir in chocolate chips, margarine and vanilla, beating until smooth. Spread warm frosting on cool brownies.

Chocolate Chip Cookies

- ½ cup butter, melted
- ½ cup firmly-packed brown sugar
- ½ cup sugar
- ½ teaspoon baking soda
- ½ teaspoon salt
- 1 egg
- 1 tablespoon vanilla
- 1½ cups all-purpose flour
- 3 6-ounce packages chocolate chips

Combine butter, brown sugar and sugar, beating until smooth. Add baking soda and salt. Beat in egg and vanilla. Add flour and chocolate chips, mixing thoroughly. Drop dough by level tablespoonfuls on baking sheet. Bake at 375° for 12 to 15 minutes. Yield: 2 to 2½ dozen.

Real Chocolate Chocolate Chip Cookies

1 cup all-purpose
flour
½ teaspoon baking
soda
Pinch of salt
½ cup sugar
½ cup unsalted
butter, softened
½ cup firmly-packed
dark brown sugar
1 egg
5 1-ounce squares
semi-sweet
chocolate, melted
1 6-ounce package
semi-sweet
chocolate chips
½ cup pecans
(optional)

Sift flour, baking soda and salt to-gether. Cream sugar and butter together until fluffy. Add egg and melted chocolate, mixing thoroughly. Add dry ingredients, mixing just until no longer visible. Stir in chips and pecans. Drop dough by tablespoonfuls on baking sheet. Bake at 350° for 10 minutes. Yield: 2 to 2½ dozen.

Variation: Peanut butter chips may be added or substituted for chocolate chips.

Chocolate Oatmeal Cookies

1 cup sugar
½ cup butter, softened
1 egg
2 1-ounce squares
chocolate, melted
¾ cup all-purpose
flour
1 teaspoon baking
powder
½ teaspoon salt
1½ cups uncooked
regular oats
1 tablespoon vanilla

Cream sugar and butter together until smooth. Add egg and beat well. Stir in melted chocolate. Sift flour, baking powder and salt together. Add dry ingredients to creamed mixture. Add oats and vanilla, mixing thoroughly. Drop dough by teaspoonfuls on baking sheet. Bake at 350° for 9 minutes. Yield: 3 to 4 dozen

Three Layer Half-Way Cookies

½ cup sugar
1½ cups firmly-packed brown sugar, divided
½ cup butter or margarine, softened
½ cup vegetable oil
2 eggs, separated
2½ cups sifted all-purpose flour
1 teaspoon baking powder
¼ teaspoon baking soda
¼ teaspoon salt
1 teaspoon vanilla
1 12-ounce package semi-sweet chocolate chips

Cream sugar, ½ cup brown sugar, butter and oil together until smooth. Add egg yolks, mixing well. Sift flour, baking powder, baking soda and salt together. Add dry ingredients and vanilla to creamed mixture to form crumb consistency. Firmly press crumbs into 12x9x2-inch greased baking pan. Spread chocolate chips on crumb layer. Beat egg whites until stiff. Fold in 1 cup brown sugar. Spread egg white mixture on chips. Bake at 375° for 20 to 25 minutes. Serve warm. Yield: 4 dozen.

Cowboy Cookies

½ cup sugar
1½ cups firmly-packed brown sugar
1 cup butter, softened
2 eggs
2 cups all-purpose flour
1 teaspoon baking soda
½ teaspoon salt
1½ teaspoons vanilla
2 cups uncooked regular oats
1 cup flaked coconut
1 12-ounce package chocolate chips

Cream sugar, brown sugar and butter together until smooth. Add eggs and beat well. Sift flour, baking soda and salt together. Add dry ingredients to creamed mixture. Stir in vanilla, oats, coconut and chocolate chips. Drop dough by teaspoonfuls on greased baking sheet. Bake at 350° for 13 to 15 minutes. Yield: 3 dozen.

Mint Surprise Cookies

Sift flour, baking soda and salt together. Cream margarine and oil together until smooth. Add sugar, brown sugar, eggs and vanilla, beating thoroughly. Add dry ingredients, mixing well. Chill dough until firm. Shape teaspoon of dough into a ball, place on baking sheet, cover with wax paper and press with bottom of drinking glass to 3-inch circle. Place mint wafer in center. Place another teaspoon ball of dough between 2 pieces of wax paper, press to 3-inch circle, remove paper and place on mint wafer. Press edges to seal. Place walnut half on top of cookie. Repeat with remaining dough, placing cookies about 2 inches apart on baking sheet. Bake at 350° for about 20 minutes. Yield: 4½ dozen.

Note: Store cookies in tightly covered container. Cookies may be frozen.

3¼ cups all-purpose flour
1 teaspoon baking soda
½ teaspoon salt
½ cup margarine, softened
½ cup vegetable oil
1 cup sugar
½ cup firmly-packed brown sugar
2 eggs, beaten
1 teaspoon vanilla
1 9½-ounce package chocolate mint wafers
English walnut halves

Fig Cookies

Combine figs and water in small saucepan. Cook over medium heat for 5 minutes. Sift flour and baking powder together. Cream brown sugar and shortening together until smooth. Add egg, vanilla, figs with cooking liquid and dry ingredients, mixing thoroughly. Shape teaspoonfuls of dough into balls, roll in coconut, top each with pecan half and place on baking sheet. Bake at 350° for 12 to 15 minutes. Yield: 2 to 2½ dozen.

1 cup chopped figs
½ cup water
1¾ cups all-purpose flour
2 teaspoons baking powder
1 cup firmly-packed brown sugar
1 cup vegetable shortening
1 egg
1 teaspoon vanilla
Flaked coconut
Pecan halves

205

Heavenly Chocolate Chip Oatmeal Cookies

2½ cups uncooked
    regular oats
1 cup sugar
1 cup firmly-packed
    brown sugar
1 cup butter, softened
3 eggs
1 teaspoon vanilla
2 cups all-purpose
    flour
½ teaspoon baking
    powder
½ teaspoon baking
    soda
½ teaspoon salt
1 12-ounce package
    chocolate chips
1 4-ounce chocolate
    candy bar, grated
1½ cups chopped
    pecans

Pour oats into blender container and process until powder consistency. Cream sugar, brown sugar and butter together until smooth. Add eggs and vanilla to creamed mixture, mixing well. Sift flour, oats, baking powder, baking soda and salt together. Add dry ingredients to creamed mixture, blending thoroughly. Stir in chocolate chips, grated chocolate and pecans. Shape dough into 1-inch balls and place 2 inches apart on ungreased baking sheet. Bake at 375° for 10 minutes. Yield: 2½ dozen.

Rock Cookies

½ **cup sugar**
¾ **cup firmly-packed brown sugar**
1 **cup butter, softened**
3 **eggs**
3 **cups all-purpose flour**
1 **cup raisins**
2 **cups chopped nuts**
1 **teaspoon baking soda**
1 **tablespoon hot water**
1 **teaspoon nutmeg**
1 **teaspoon ground cloves**
1 **teaspoon ginger**
1 **teaspoon cinnamon**
1 **teaspoon allspice**

Cream sugar, brown sugar and butter together until smooth. Add eggs and beat well. Stir in flour, raisins and nuts. Dissolve baking soda in hot water. Add baking soda liquid, nutmeg, cloves, ginger, cinnamon and allspice to dough. Drop dough by rounded teaspoonfuls on greased baking sheet. Bake at 375° for about 10 minutes. Yield: 4 to 5 dozen.

Ginger Cookies

1 **cup molasses**
2 **cups firmly-packed brown sugar**
2 **cups vegetable shortening**
2 **cups milk**
2 **tablespoons ginger**
2 **tablespoons cinnamon**
3 **eggs**
1 **tablespoon vanilla**
2 **teaspoons baking soda**
6 **cups all-purpose flour**

Combine molasses, brown sugar and shortening, mixing well. Add milk. Stir in ginger, cinnamon, eggs and vanilla. Add baking soda and flour, blending thoroughly to form soft dough. Chill overnight. Press dough to ½-inch thickness on lightly-floured surface. Cut with cookie cutter and place on baking sheet. Bake at 375° for 20 to 12 minutes. Yield: 5 to 6 dozen.

Lemon Iced Bars

Crust

1½ cups all-purpose
  flour
½ cup firmly-packed
  brown sugar
½ cup butter

Combine flour and brown sugar. Add butter and mix thoroughly. Press mixture into 13x9x2-inch baking pan. Bake at 275° for 10 minutes.

Filling

2 eggs, beaten
1 cup firmly-packed
  brown sugar
1½ cups flaked coconut
½ cup chopped nuts
2 tablespoons flour
½ teaspoon baking
  powder
¼ teaspoon salt
½ teaspoon vanilla

Combine eggs, brown sugar, coconut, nuts, flour, baking powder, salt and vanilla, beating well. Pour mixture on baked crust. Bake at 350° for 20 minutes. Spread frosting on warm bar surface. Cool before cutting. Yield: 4 dozen.

Frosting

1 tablespoon melted
  butter
1 tablespoon lemon
  juice
1 cup sifted powdered
  sugar

Combine butter and lemon juice. Blend in sugar, mixing until smooth. Spread frosting on warm bars.

Healthy Oatmeal Cookies

Combine oil and honey, beating until well blended. Add egg and vanilla or lemon extract. Combine flour, baking soda, cinnamon and nutmeg. Add dry ingredients to egg mixture, mixing thoroughly. Stir in oats, raisins, walnuts and carob chips. Drop dough by tablespoonfuls on baking sheet, pressing to slightly flatten. Bake at 375° for 9 to 10 minutes. Cool on sheet for 1 minute before removing. Yield: 3 dozen.

- 1 cup canola oil
- ¾ cup honey
- 1 egg
- 1 teaspoon vanilla or lemon extract
- 1½ cups whole wheat flour
- 1 teaspoon baking soda
- 1 teaspoon cinnamon
- ½ teaspoon nutmeg
- 3½ cups uncooked regular oats
- ½ cup raisins (optional)
- ½ cup chopped walnuts (optional)
- ½ cup unsweetened carob chips

Almond Sugar Cookies

Cream sugar, margarine and oil together until fluffy. Add eggs, vanilla and almond extract. Sift flour, baking soda, cream of tartar and salt together. Add dry ingredients to creamed mixture. Chill dough for at least 1 hour. Shape dough into small balls, place on baking sheet and press with bottom of drinking glass dipped in sugar. Bake at 350° for 10 minutes or until lightly browned. Yield: 4 dozen.

- 2 cups sugar
- 1 cup margarine, softened
- 1 cup vegetable oil
- 2 eggs
- 1 teaspoon vanilla
- 1 teaspoon almond extract
- 4½ cups all-purpose flour
- 2 teaspoons baking soda
- 2 teaspoons cream of tartar
- 1 teaspoon salt

Zucchini Cookies

1 cup sugar
½ cup margarine,
  softened
1 egg
2 cups all-purpose
  flour
1 teaspoon baking
  soda
½ teaspoon salt
1 teaspoon cinnamon
½ teaspoon cloves
1 cup grated zucchini
1 cup raisins
  (optional)
1 cup chopped nuts

Cream sugar, margarine and egg together until smooth. Sift flour, baking soda, salt, cinnamon and cloves together. Add dry ingredients to creamed mixture. Stir in zucchini, raisins and nuts. Drop dough by teaspoonfuls on baking sheet. Bake at 375° for 12 to 15 minutes. Yield: 2 to 2½ dozen.

Peanut Butter Bars

1 cup sugar
1 cup firmly-packed
  brown sugar
1 cup margarine,
  softened
1 cup peanut butter
2 eggs, well beaten
1 tablespoon milk
½ teaspoon salt
1½ cups sifted all-
  purpose flour
½ teaspoon baking
  soda
½ cup uncooked
  regular oats
1½ teaspoons vanilla
½ teaspoon almond
  extract
1 6-ounce package
  chocolate chips

Cream sugar, brown sugar, margarine and peanut butter together until smooth. Add eggs, milk and salt, beating until light and fluffy. Sift flour and baking soda together. Add dry ingredients to peanut butter mixture. Stir oats, vanilla and almond extract into dough. Spread dough on 15x10x1-inch baking sheet. Sprinkle chocolate chips on dough. Bake at 325° for 20 to 25 minutes; center may not appear firm but do not over bake. Cool before cutting into bars. Store in airtight container. Yield: 3 dozen.

Pumpkin Bars

Bars

    4 eggs
    1 cup vegetable oil
    1 16-ounce can
       pumpkin
 1⅔ cups sugar
    2 cups all-purpose
       flour
    2 teaspoons baking
       powder
    1 teaspoon baking
       soda
    1 teaspoon salt
    2 teaspoons
       cinnamon

Using electric mixer, beat eggs, oil, pumpkin and sugar together until light and fluffy. Sift flour, baking powder, baking soda, salt and cinnamon together. Add dry ingredients to pumpkin mixture and mix thoroughly. Pour batter into ungreased 15x10x1-inch baking sheet. Bake at 350° for 25 to 30 minutes. Cool before frosting. Cut into bars. Yield: 3 dozen.

Cream Cheese Frosting

    1 3-ounce package
       cream cheese,
       softened
 ½ cup butter or
       margarine, softened
    1 teaspoon vanilla
    2 cups sifted
       powdered sugar

Combine cream cheese and butter, beating until smooth. Stir in vanilla. Gradually add powdered sugar, beating well after each addition. Spread frosting on cooled bars.

211

Walnut Dream Bars

Crust
- ½ **cup firmly-packed light brown sugar**
- 1 **cup sifted all-purpose flour**
- ½ **cup butter, softened**

Combine brown sugar, flour and butter, mixing with hands to form smooth dough. Spread evenly in 8x8x2-inch baking pan. Bake at 350° until golden brown. Cool before adding filling.

Filling
- 2 **eggs**
- 1 **cup firmly-packed light brown sugar**
- 1 **teaspoon vanilla**
- 1 **tablespoon all-purpose flour**
- ¼ **teaspoon baking powder**
- ½ **teaspoon salt**
- 1½ **cups chopped walnuts**

Using electric mixer, beat eggs until light. Gradually add sugar, beating well. Add vanilla, flour, baking powder and salt. Fold walnuts into egg mixture. Spread filling on cooled crust. Bake at 375° for 20 minutes or until browned. Yield: 1¼ dozen.

Dibble Dabble Cake

- 1½ **cups vegetable oil**
- 2 **cups sugar**
- 3 **eggs**
- 2 **tablespoons cinnamon**
- 1 **teaspoon vanilla**
- ½ **teaspoon salt**
- 1 **teaspoon baking soda**
- 3 **cups diced apples**
- 1 **cup chopped nuts**
- 1 **cup raisins**
- 3 **cups all-purpose flour**

Combine oil and sugar. Add, in order listed, eggs, cinnamon, vanilla, salt, backing soda, apples, nuts and raisins, mixing well after each addition. Gradually add flour, mixing by hand. Pour batter into 10-inch fluted tube pan. Bake at 350° for 1 hour. Let cool in pan for 10 minutes before inverting on wire rack. Yield: 12 to 16 servings.

Apricot Crumble Cake

Cake

1¼ cups sugar
1 8-ounce package cream cheese, softened
½ cup margarine, softened
2 eggs
¼ cup milk
1 teaspoon vanilla
2 cups sifted cake flour
1 teaspoon baking powder
½ teaspoon baking soda
¼ teaspoon salt
1 10-ounce jar apricot or peach preserves

Topping

2 cups shredded coconut
⅔ cup firmly-packed brown sugar
1 teaspoon cinnamon
⅓ cup margarine, melted

Cream sugar, cream cheese and margarine together until well blended. Add eggs, milk and vanilla, mixing thoroughly. Sift flour, baking powder, baking soda and salt together. Add dry ingredients to creamed mixture. Pour ½ of batter into greased and floured 13x9x2-inch baking pan. Spoon preserves evenly on batter. Pour remaining batter on preserves. Bake at 350° for 35 to 40 minutes. Spread topping on hot cake and broil until golden brown. Yield: 16 to 20 servings.

Combine coconut, brown sugar, cinnamon and margarine, mixing thoroughly. Spread mixture on hot cake. Broil until golden brown.

Tropical Banana Cake

Cake

1 18½-ounce package white cake mix
½ cup vegetable oil
4 eggs
¼ cup milk
1 teaspoon vanilla
1 teaspoon banana extract
¼ teaspoon nutmeg
3 bananas, mashed

Combine cake mix, oil, eggs, milk, vanilla, banana extract and nutmeg. Using electric mixer, beat at medium speed for 3 minutes. Fold bananas into batter. Pour batter into 2 greased and floured 9-inch round baking pans. Bake at 350° for 25 to 30 minutes. Spread cooled layer with frosting, add second layer and spread frosting on top and sides of assembled cake. Yield: 12 to 16 servings.

Tropical Frosting

2 3-ounce packages cream cheese, softened
1 tablespoon butter, softened
1 16-ounce package powdered sugar
½ teaspoon ginger
¼ teaspoon nutmeg
2 tablespoons whipping cream
1 teaspoon vanilla extract

Combine cream cheese and butter, beating until light and fluffy. Gradually add sugar, beating until smooth. Stir in ginger, nutmeg, cream and vanilla extract, beating until well blended. Spread frosting on cooled cake layer, add second layer and frost top and sides of cake.

Banana Snack Cake

Cream sugar, margarine and eggs together until smooth. Add buttermilk, bananas and vanilla, blending thoroughly. Stir in flour, baking soda, salt and oats, mixing well. Fold in chocolate chips. Spread batter in greased 13x9x2-inch baking pan. Sprinkle pecans on batter. Bake at 350° for 30 to 35 minutes. Yield: 16 to 20 servings.

1 cup sugar
1 cup margarine or butter
2 eggs
1 cup buttermilk
1 cup mashed ripe bananas
1 teaspoon vanilla
2 cups all-purpose flour
1½ teaspoons baking soda
½ teaspoon salt
1 cup uncooked quick-cooking oats
1 6-ounce package semi-sweet chocolate chips
½ cup chopped pecans

Cherry Cake

Cream sugar, butter and cream cheese together until smooth. Add eggs and beat well. Stir in flour, baking powder, vanilla, cherries and raisins. Spread batter in 10-inch fluted tube pan. Bake at 300° for 1½ hours. Yield: 16 servings.

1½ cups sugar
1 cup butter, softened
1 8-ounce package cream cheese, softened
4 eggs
2¼ cups all-purpose flour
1½ teaspoons baking powder
1½ teaspoons vanilla
2 cups cherries
2 cups golden raisins

14 Carat Cake

Cake

    2 **cups sifted all-purpose flour**
    2 **teaspoons baking powder**
  1½ **teaspoons baking soda**
  1½ **teaspoons salt**
    2 **teaspoons cinnamon**
    2 **cups sugar**
  1½ **cups vegetable oil**
    4 **eggs**
    2 **cups finely grated carrots**
    1 **8-ounce can crushed pineapple, drained**
  ½ **cup chopped nuts**
    1 **3½-ounce can flaked coconut (optional)**

Sift flour, baking powder, baking soda, salt and cinnamon together. Add sugar, oil and eggs to dry ingredients, mixing thoroughly. Add carrots, pineapple, nuts and coconut, blending well. Pour batter into 3 greased and floured 9-inch round baking pans. Bake at 350° for 35 to 40 minutes. Spread frosting on cooled cake layer, add second layer, spread with frosting, and top with third layer, spreading frosting on top and sides of assembled cake. Yield: 12 to 16 servings.

Cream Cheese Frosting

  ½ **cup butter or margarine, softened**
    1 **8-ounce package cream cheese, softened**
    1 **teaspoon vanilla**
    1 **16-ounce package powdered sugar, sifted**

Cream butter, cream cheese and vanilla together until smooth. Gradually add sugar, beating well after each addition. If frosting too thick to spread, add a small amount of milk. Spread frosting on cooled cake layers.

Chocolate Mayonnaise Cake

Sift flour, sugar, cocoa, baking powder and baking soda together. Add mayonnaise, mixing well. Gradually add water and vanilla, mixing until smooth and well blended. Pour batter into greased 9x9x2-inch baking pan. Bake at 350° for 40 to 45 minutes or until wooden pick inserted near center comes out clean. Cool cake in pan. Yield: 9 servings.

2 cups unsifted all-purpose flour
1 cup sugar
½ cup cocoa
1½ teaspoons baking powder
1 teaspoon baking soda
1 cup mayonnaise
1 cup water
1 teaspoon vanilla

Scotch Cake

Cake

Sift flour and sugar together. Combine margarine, shortening, water and cocoa in saucepan. Bring to a broil. Add liquid mixture to dry ingredients. Stir in buttermilk, baking soda, salt, vanilla and eggs, mixing thoroughly. Pour batter into 2 greased and floured 9-inch round baking pans. Bake at 350° for 20 to 30 minutes. Spread frosting on cooled cake layer, add second layer and spread frosting on sides and top of assembled cake. Yield: 12 to 16 servings.

2 cups all-purpose flour
2 cups sugar
½ cup margarine
½ cup vegetable shortening
1 cup water
¼ cup cocoa
½ cup buttermilk
1 teaspoon baking soda
½ teaspoon salt
1 teaspoon vanilla
2 eggs, lightly beaten

Scotch Cake Frosting

Sift powdered sugar and cocoa together. Add sour cream, 1 tablespoon at a time, until frosting is spreading consistency. Beat in margarine and vanilla until smooth and fluffy. Spread frosting on cooled cake layers.

1 16-ounce package powdered sugar
½ cup cocoa
Sour cream
¾ cup melted margarine
1 teaspoon vanilla

217

Easy Fluffy Chocolate Cake

2 cups sugar, divided
1 cup vegetable oil
1 cup sour cream
1 teaspoon vanilla
2 cups all-purpose flour
⅓ cup cocoa
1 tablespoon baking soda
¼ teaspoon salt
1 cup boiling water
Powdered sugar

Combine 1 cup sugar, oil, sour cream and vanilla, beating until well blended. Add flour, 1 cup sugar, cocoa, baking soda and salt, beating well. Add water, blending thoroughly. Pour batter into 2 9-inch round baking pans or one 13x9x2-inch baking pan. Bake at 350° for 40 minutes or until wooden pick inserted near center comes out clean. Sprinkle powdered sugar on top of warm cake. Yield: 16 to 20 servings.

Hot Fudge Cake

1 cup all-purpose flour
¾ cup sugar
¼ cup plus 2 tablespoons cocoa, divided
2 teaspoons baking powder
¼ teaspoon salt
½ cup milk
2 tablespoons canola oil
1 teaspoon vanilla
½ to 1 cup chopped nuts
1 cup firmly-packed brown sugar
1¾ cups very hot tap water

Combine flour, sugar, 2 tablespoons cocoa, baking powder and salt in ungreased 9x9x2-inch baking pan or dish. Add milk, oil and vanilla, mixing with fork until smooth. Stir in nuts. Sprinkle brown sugar and ¼ cup cocoa on batter. Pour hot water over batter; do not stir. Bake at 350° for 40 minutes. Spoon warm cake into individual dessert dishes and add scoops of ice cream. Spoon any remaining sauce from pan on each serving. Yield: 9 servings.

Southern Georgia Chocolate Pound Cake

Sift flour, sugar, cocoa, baking powder and salt together. Add margarine, mixing well. Add milk and vanilla, blending thoroughly. Add eggs and half and half. Pour batter into greased and floured 10-inch tube pan. Bake at 325° for 1½ hours. Cool in pan for 10 minutes, then invert on wire rack to complete cooling. Yield: 12 to 16 servings.

- 3 cups all-purpose flour
- 3 cups sugar
- ½ cup cocoa
- 1 tablespoon baking powder
- ½ teaspoon salt
- 1 cup margarine, softened
- 1½ cups milk
- 1 tablespoon vanilla
- 3 eggs
- ¼ cup half and half

Chocolate Chip Pound Cake

Combine cake mix and pudding mixes. Add oil, water, eggs, vanilla and almond extract, beating well. Stir in chocolate chips. Pour batter into greased and floured 10-inch fluted tube pan. Bake at 350° for 1 hour. Cool in pan for 10 minutes, then invert on wire rack. Yield: 12 to 16 servings.

- 1 18½-ounce package yellow cake mix
- 1 3¾-ounce package instant chocolate pudding mix
- 1 3¾-ounce package instant vanilla pudding mix
- ½ cup oil
- 1¼ cups water
- 4 eggs
- 1 teaspoon vanilla
- 1 teaspoon almond extract
- 1 6-ounce package chocolate chips

Red Velvet Cake

Cake

- 2 cups sugar
- 1½ cups vegetable oil
- 2 eggs
- 2 drops red food coloring
- 1 cup buttermilk
- 1 teaspoon vinegar
- 1 teaspoon vanilla
- 2½ cups all-purpose flour
- 2 teaspoons cocoa
- 1 teaspoon baking soda
- 1 teaspoon salt

Cream sugar, oil, eggs, food coloring, buttermilk, vinegar and vanilla together until smooth. Add flour, cocoa, baking soda and salt, mixing thoroughly. Pour batter into 3 9-inch round baking pans. Bake at 350° for 30 minutes. Spread frosting on cooled cake layer, add second layer, spread with frosting, top with third layer and spread frosting on top and sides of assembled cake. Yield: 12 to 16 servings.

Frosting

- 1 8-ounce package cream cheese, softened
- 2⅓ tablespoons margarine, softened
- 1 16-ounce package powdered sugar
- ½ cup ground pecans

Combine cream cheese, margarine and powdered sugar, creaming until smooth. Add pecans. Spread frosting on cooled cake layers.

Old Fashioned Coconut Cake

Cream sugar and oil together until smooth. Add eggs, blending well. Sift flour, baking powder, baking soda and salt together. Alternately add dry ingredients and buttermilk to creamed mixture, mixing well after each addition. Stir in vanilla. Pour batter into 3 9-inch round baking pans. Bake at 350° for 30 to 35 minutes. Spread Coconut Pecan Frosting (page 233) on cooled cake layers. Yield: 12 to 16 servings.

2 cups sugar
1 cup vegetable oil
3 eggs
2 cups all-purpose flour
1 teaspoon baking powder
½ teaspoon baking soda
½ teaspoon salt
1 cup buttermilk
1 teaspoon vanilla

Honey Cake

(Lekach)

Beat egg whites until stiff and chill until ready to use. Cream brown sugar, oil, honey and egg yolks together until smooth. Sift flour, baking powder, baking soda, salt, cinnamon and cloves together. Combine orange juice and tea. Alternately add dry ingredients and liquid mixture to creamed mixture, mixing well. Fold egg whites into batter. Pour batter into 2 9x5x3-inch loaf pans lined with oiled wax paper. Bake at 325° for 1 hour. Cool loaves in pans for 10 minutes, then invert on wire rack. Yield: 20 to 24 servings.

4 eggs, separated
1 cup firmly-packed brown sugar
½ cup vegetable oil
1 cup honey
3 cups sifted all-purpose flour
2 teaspoons baking powder
½ teaspoon baking soda
½ teaspoon salt
½ teaspoon cinnamon
½ teaspoon ground cloves (optional)
½ cup orange juice
½ cup strong tea

Japanese Fruit Cake

Cake

2 cups sugar
1 cup butter, softened
4 eggs
3 cups all-purpose
flour
2 teaspoons baking
powder
1 cup milk
1 teaspoon vanilla
1 teaspoon ground
cloves
1 teaspoon cinnamon
½ cup raisins
½ cup chopped pecans

Cream sugar and butter together until smooth. Add eggs, 1 at a time, beating well after each addition. Combine flour and baking powder. Alternately add dry ingredients and milk to creamed mixture, beginning and ending with dry ingredients. Stir in vanilla. Divide batter into 2 portions. Add spices, raisins and pecans to one portion. Pour spiced batter into 2 greased and floured 9-inch round baking pans. Pour plain batter into 2 greased and floured 9-inch round baking pans. Bake at 350° for 20 to 25 minutes or until wooden pick inserted near center comes out clean. Cool cake in pans for 10 minutes, then invert on wire rack. Pierce each layer with fork tines at 1-inch intervals. Spread frosting on cooled spice layer, add plain layer, spread with frosting, and repeat with remaining layers, spreading frosting on top and sides of assembled cake. Yield: 12 to 16 servings.

Japanese Fruit Cake Frosting

2½ cups sugar
3 tablespoons all-purpose flour
½ teaspoon salt
1 cup boiling water
1½ tablespoons grated lemon peel
¼ cup fresh lemon juice
4½ cups grated coconut

Combine sugar, flour and salt in saucepan. Add water, lemon peel and juice and coconut. Bring to a boil over medium heat and cook, stirring constantly, for 5 minutes or until thickened. Cool frosting, stirring occasionally, before spreading on cooled cake layers.

Cola Cake

Cake

 2 **cups all-purpose flour**
 2 **cups sugar**
 1 **teaspoon baking soda**
 1 **cup margarine**
 1 **cup cola-flavored carbonated drink**
 3 **tablespoons cocoa**
 2 **eggs, beaten**
 ½ **cup buttermilk**
 1 **teaspoon vanilla**
 1½ **cups miniature marshmallows**

Combine flour, sugar and baking soda in mixing bowl. Combine margarine, cola and cocoa in saucepan. Bring to a boil. Pour cola liquid into dry ingredients and mix well. Add eggs, buttermilk and vanilla, blending thoroughly. Fold marshmallows into batter. Pour batter into greased 13x9x2-inch baking pan. Bake at 350° for 30 to 40 minutes. Spread frosting on hot cake. Yield: 16 to 20 servings.

Cola Frosting

 ½ **cup margarine**
 6 **tablespoons cola-flavored carbonated drink**
 3 **tablespoons cocoa**
 1 **16-ounce package powdered sugar**
 1 **teaspoon vanilla**
 1 **cup chopped pecans**

Combine margarine, cola and cocoa in saucepan. Bring to a boil. Add powdered sugar and beat well. Stir in vanilla and pecans. Spread frosting on hot cake.

Italian Cream Cake

Cake

- 2 **cups sugar**
- ½ **cup margarine, softened**
- ½ **cup vegetable shortening**
- 5 **eggs, divided**
- 2 **cups all-purpose flour**
- 1 **teaspoon baking soda**
- 1 **cup buttermilk**
- 1 **teaspoon vanilla**
- 1 **3½-ounce can flaked coconut**
- 1 **cup chopped nuts**

Cream sugar, margarine and shortening together until smooth. Add egg yolks, beating well. Combine flour and baking soda. Alternately add dry ingredients and buttermilk to creamed mixture. Stir in vanilla. Add coconut and nuts. Beat egg whites until stiff. Fold egg whites into batter. Spread batter in 3 greased 8-inch round baking pans. Bake at 350° for 25 minutes or until wooden pick inserted near center comes out clean. Spread frosting on cooled cake layer, add second layer, spread with frosting, and top with third layer, spreading frosting on top and sides of assembled cake. Yield: 12 to 16 servings.

Cream Cheese Frosting

- 1 **8-ounce package cream cheese, softened**
- ¼ **cup margarine, softened**
- 1 **16-ounce package powdered sugar**
- 1 **teaspoon vanilla**
- ½ **cup chopped pecans**

Combine cream cheese and margarine, creaming until smooth. Add powdered sugar, mixing thoroughly. Add vanilla and beat until smooth. Stir in nuts. Spread frosting on cooled cake layers.

Lemon-Lime Cake

Cake

Combine cake mix and pudding mix. Add oil, eggs and lemon-lime drink, mixing well. Pour batter into greased and floured 13x9x2-inch baking pan. Bake at 350° for 35 to 45 minutes. Spread frosting on cooled cake. Yield: 16 to 20 servings.

1 18½-ounce package lemon cake mix
1 3¾-ounce package lemon instant pudding mix
¾ cup vegetable oil
4 eggs
1½ cups lemon-lime flavored carbonated drink

Frosting

Combine sugar, Milnot, butter, egg yolks and vanilla in saucepan. Cook for several minutes. Remove from heat and add pineapple, coconut and nuts. Spread frosting on cooled cake.

1 cup sugar
1 cup Milnot
½ cup butter
3 egg yolks
1 teaspoon vanilla
1 8-ounce can crushed pineapple, drained
1 3½-ounce can flaked coconut
½ cup chopped nuts

Mardi Gras Cake

Melt margarine in 13x9x2-inch baking pan or 12-inch oven-proof skillet. Add brown sugar, mixing well. Arrange fruit on sugar mixture. Prepare cake mix according to package directions, using 1 cup water and reserved fruit syrup for liquid. Pour batter over fruit. Bake at 350° for 45 to 50 minutes. Cool in pan for 5 minutes, then invert on serving dish. Serve warm or cold. Yield: 16 to 20 servings.

½ cup margarine or butter
1 cup firmly-packed brown sugar
1 30-ounce can fruit cocktail, drained and ⅓ cup syrup reserved
1 18½-ounce package lemon cake mix
1 cup water

Lemon Cake

Cake

>   1 3-ounce package
>   lemon gelatin
>   ¾ cup boiling water
>   ¾ cup vegetable oil
>   4 eggs
>   4 teaspoons lemon
>   extract
>   1 18½-ounce package
>   yellow cake mix

Dissolve gelatin in boiling water. Cool to lukewarm. Add oil, eggs and lemon extract. Add cake mix, mixing thoroughly. Pour batter into 10-inch tube pan prepared with non-stick vegetable spray. Bake at 350° for 50 minutes. Pour glaze over hot cake in pan; cool for 2 hours before removing from pan. Yield: 12 to 16 servings.

Glaze

>   1 6-ounce can frozen
>   lemonade
>   concentrate,
>   thawed
>   ¾ cup sugar

Combine lemonade and sugar, mixing well. Pour glaze over hot cake in pan.

Pumpkin Pie Cake

>   1 18½-ounce package
>   yellow cake mix
>   1 egg
>   ¼ cup margarine,
>   melted
>   3½ cups canned
>   pumpkin
>   1¼ cups sugar, divided
>   2 teaspoons
>   cinnamon
>   ⅔ cup evaporated
>   milk
>   3 eggs
>   2 tablespoons
>   margarine
>   ½ cup chopped nuts
>   (optional)

Reserve 1 cup cake mix. Combine remaining cake mix, egg and melted margarine, mixing thoroughly. Press mixture into 13x9x2-inch baking pan. Combine pumpkin, ½ cup sugar, cinnamon, milk and eggs, blending well. Pour batter over cake mix layer. Combine reserved cake mix, 2 tablespoons margarine, ¾ cup sugar and nuts. Sprinkle mixture on pumpkin layer. Bake at 350° for 55 minutes. Yield: 16 to 20 servings.

Pumpkin Cake Roll

Cake

Using electric mixer, beat eggs at high speed for 5 minutes. Gradually add sugar, beating well. Stir in pumpkin and lemon juice. Combine flour, baking powder, salt, cinnamon, ginger and nutmeg. Fold dry ingredients into pumpkin mixture. Spread batter on greased and floured 15x10x1-inch baking sheet. Sprinkle nuts on batter. Bake at 375° for 15 minutes. Invert cake on towel sprinkled with powdered sugar. Starting at narrow end, roll towel and cake together. Place, seam side down, on wire rack to cool. To fill, unroll cake, spread filling to within 1 inch of edges, reroll and chill. Cut into 1-inch slices to serve. Yield: 12 to 15 servings.

3 eggs
1 cup sugar
⅔ cup canned pumpkin
1 teaspoon lemon juice
¾ cup all-purpose flour
1 teaspoon baking powder
½ teaspoon salt
2 teaspoons cinnamon
1 teaspoon ginger
½ teaspoon nutmeg
1 cup chopped walnuts

Filling

Cream powdered sugar, cream cheese, butter and vanilla until smooth. Spread filling on cake.

1 cup sifted powdered sugar
1 8-ounce package cream cheese, softened
¼ cup butter, softened
½ teaspoon vanilla

Oatmeal Cake

Cake

1½ cups boiling water
1 cup uncooked quick-cooking oats
1 cup sugar
1 cup firmly-packed brown sugar
½ cup margarine
2 eggs
1 teaspoon vanilla
1½ cups all-purpose flour
1 teaspoon baking soda
½ teaspoon salt
¾ teaspoon cinnamon
¼ teaspoon nutmeg

Pour boiling water on oats and let stand for 20 minutes. Cream sugar, brown sugar and margarine together until fluffy. Add eggs and vanilla, blending thoroughly. Add oatmeal mixture and mix well. Sift flour, baking soda, salt, cinnamon and nutmeg together. Add dry ingredients to creamed mixture. Spread batter in greased and flour 13x9x2-inch baking pan. Bake at 350° for 50 to 55 minutes. Spread frosting on warm cake and broil until bubbly. Yield: 16 to 20 servings.

Frosting

½ cup firmly-packed brown sugar
¼ cup margarine
3 tablespoons milk
⅓ cup chopped nuts
¾ cup flaked coconut

Combine brown sugar, margarine, milk, nuts and coconut. Spread on warm cake and broil until bubbly.

Sour Cream Pound Cake

Cream sugar, margarine and shortening together until fluffy. Add eggs, 1 at a time, beating well after each addition. Sift flour and baking soda together. Alternately add dry ingredients and milk and sour cream to creamed mixture, mixing well. Stir in vanilla and lemon extract. Pour batter into greased and floured 10-inch fluted tube pan. Bake at 300° for 1½ hours. Cool in pan for 10 minutes, then invert on wire rack. Yield: 12 to 16 servings.

3 cups sugar
1 cup margarine, softened
½ cup vegetable shortening
5 eggs
3 cups sifted cake flour
¼ teaspoon baking soda
½ cup milk
1 cup sour cream
1 teaspoon vanilla
1 teaspoon lemon extract

Southern Cake

Combine cake mix, pudding mix and sugar. Make a well in center of dry ingredients. Add oil and sour cream, blending thoroughly. Add eggs, 1 at a time, beating well after each addition. Pour ½ of batter into greased and floured 10-inch tube pan. Combine brown sugar, cinnamon and pecans. Sprinkle mixture on batter and top with remaining batter. Bake at 350° for 45 minutes. Cool in pan for 10 minutes, then invert on wire rack. Serve plain or with glaze. Yield: 12 to 16 servings.

1 18½-ounce package butter cake mix
1 3¾-ounce package instant vanilla pudding mix
½ cup sugar
¾ cup vegetable oil
1 cup sour cream
4 eggs
1 tablespoon brown sugar
2 teaspoons cinnamon
½ cup crushed pecans

Spice Cake

Cake

2 cups firmly-packed brown sugar

½ cup margarine, softened

3 eggs

½ teaspoon salt

1 teaspoon baking powder

1 teaspoon baking soda

1 teaspoon cinnamon

1 teaspoon ground cloves

2⅔ cups all-purpose flour

1 cup sour cream or milk

Cream brown sugar and margarine together until smooth. Add eggs, beating well. Stir in salt, baking powder, baking soda, cinnamon and cloves, mixing thoroughly. Alternately add flour and sour cream, blending well after each addition. Pour batter into 13x9x2-inch baking pan. Bake at 350° for 35 to 40 minutes. Spread cooled cake with frosting. Yield: 16 to 20 servings.

Creamy Caramel Frosting

2 cups firmly-packed brown sugar

½ cup margarine

½ cup evaporated milk

1 teaspoon vanilla

Combine brown sugar, margarine and milk in saucepan. Bring to a boil and cook for 1 minutes. Stir in vanilla. Cool, stirring occasionally, before spreading on cooled cake.

Texas Pecan Cake

Cream sugar and butter until fluffy. Add eggs, 1 at a time, beating well after each addition. Stir in lemon extract. Sift flour and baking powder together 3 times. Add pecans and raisins to dry ingredients. Add creamed mixture to dry ingredients and mix well. Spread batter in foil-lined 10-inch tube pan or 2 9x5x3-inch loaf pans. Bake at 275° for 1½ hours. Yield: 20 to 24 servings.

2 cups sugar
2 cups butter or margarine, softened
6 eggs
1 tablespoon lemon extract
4 cups all-purpose flour
1½ teaspoons baking powder
4 cups pecan halves
1 16-ounce package golden raisins

Hot Peach Roll

Melt butter in shallow baking pan. Combine flour, salt, shortening and milk, mixing until dough forms. On lightly floured surface, roll dough to rectangle shape. Place peaches on dough and roll, jelly roll fashion, as tightly as possible. Cut roll in ¾-inch slices to form 12 pieces. Place rolls, cut side down, in butter in pan. Combine water and sugar in saucepan. Bring to a boil and pour over rolls. Bake at 375° for 45 minutes; do not overbake. Yield: 12 servings.

½ cup butter or margarine
1 cup all-purpose flour
Pinch of salt
⅓ cup vegetable shortening
⅓ cup milk
6 fresh peaches, peeled and sliced
1½ cups water
1½ cups sugar

Mocha Cake

Cake

1 tablespoon instant
   coffee powder
½ cup boiling water
5 eggs, separated
1 cup sugar
1 teaspoon vanilla
1 cup all-purpose
   flour
1 teaspoon baking
   powder
Pinch of salt

Dissolve coffee in boiling water. Cream egg yolks until light yellow. Add sugar, vanilla and coffee, beating thoroughly. Sift flour, baking powder and salt together. Add to egg mixture. Beat egg whites until stiff and fold into batter. Spread batter in 2 9-inch baking pans. Bake at 350° for 25 minutes. Spread frosting on cooled cake layer, add second layer and spread frosting on top and sides of assembled cake. Yield: 12 to 16 servings.

Frosting

½ pint whipping
   cream
1⅔ cups powdered
   sugar
1 teaspoon vanilla
2 teaspoons instant
   coffee powder

Whip cream until slightly thickened. Add sugar, vanilla and coffee, beating until firm peaks form. Spread frosting on cooled cake layers.

Mexican Wedding Cake

Cake

   2 **cups all-purpose flour**
   2 **cups sugar**
   1 **teaspoon baking soda**
   1 **15-ounce can crushed pineapple, undrained**
   ½ **cup chopped nuts**

Combine flour, sugar and soda. Add pineapple and nuts, mixing well. Spread batter in greased and floured 13x9x2-inch baking pan. Bake at 350° for 30 to 35 minutes. Spread frosting on cooled cake. Yield: 16 to 20 servings.

Frosting

   ¾ **cup sugar**
   ½ **cup margarine, softened**
   1 **8-ounce package cream cheese, softened**
   1 **teaspoon vanilla**
   ½ **cup chopped nuts**

Cream sugar, margarine and cream cheese together until fluffy. Add vanilla and nuts. Spread frosting on cooled cake.

Coconut Pecan Frosting

   1 **cup sugar**
   1 **cup evaporated milk or half and half**
   3 **egg yolks**
   ½ **cup margarine**
   1 **teaspoon vanilla**
   1 **3½-ounce can flaked coconut**
   1 **cup broken pecans**

Combine sugar, milk, egg yolks and margarine in saucepan. Cook over low to medium heat until thickened. Simmer, stirring frequently, for 30 to 45 minutes. Stir in vanilla, coconut and pecans. Beat until cool and spreading consistency. Yield: for 2 or 3 layer cake

Fudge Frosting

2 cups sugar
¼ teaspoon salt
¼ cup light corn
  syrup
½ cup milk
½ cup vegetable
  shortening
4 teaspoons cocoa
1 teaspoon vanilla
1 tablespoon
  margarine

Combine sugar, salt, syrup, milk, shortening and cocoa in saucepan. Cook over low heat, stirring constantly, until shortening is melted. Bring to a boil and cook for 1 minute. Remove from heat, add vanilla and continue stirring. When gloss appears, add margarine and mix until spreading consistency. Yield: for 2 layer cake.

Whipped Cream Frosting

3 cups whipping
  cream
1 3¾-ounce package
  instant vanilla
  pudding mix
1 8-ounce can
  crushed pineapple
  in juice, drained

Combine cream, pudding mix and pineapple, whipping until spreading consistency. Yield: for 2 layer cake.

Miniature Cheesecakes

⅔ cup sugar
3 8-ounce packages
  cream cheese,
  softened
3 eggs
1 teaspoon vanilla
24 vanilla wafers
1 21-ounce can cherry
  or blueberry pie
  filling

Cream sugar, cream cheese, eggs and vanilla together until smooth. Place vanilla wafer, flat side down, in paper-lined cups of muffin pans. Spoon cream cheese mixture into cup, filling ¾ full. Bake at 350° for 15 to 20 minutes. Cool. Spoon pie filling on each cheesecake. Store in refrigerator. Yield: 2 dozen.

Candy Crunch Cake

Combine sugar, coffee, syrup and water in saucepan. Cook to hard crack stage or 285° on candy thermometer. Remove from heat, add soda and stir vigorously just until mixture blends and leaves pan sides. Pour mixture on aluminum foil sheet; do not spread or stir. Let stand to cool and harden, then crush to form crumbs. Cut cake into 2 layers. Combine part of candy crumbs with whipped topping and spread over first cake layer, sprinkling with some larger pieces of candy. Add second layer and spread top and sides with whipped topping. Sprinkle with remaining candy and almonds. Chill for 2 hours or longer before serving. Yield: 12 to 16 servings.

¾ teaspoon sugar
½ teaspoon instant coffee powder
2 tablespoons light corn syrup
2 tablespoons water
1½ teaspoons sifted baking soda
1 angel food cake Whipped topping Slivered almonds, toasted

Popcorn Cake

Combine margarine and oil in saucepan. Add marshmallows and cook until melted and well blended. Pour marshmallow mixture on popped corn and peanuts in large pan. Add candy and mix to distribute evenly. Press popcorn mixture in 13x9x2-inch baking pan or 10-inch tube pan prepared with non-stick vegetable spray. Yield: 20 servings.

½ cup margarine
¼ cup vegetable oil
1 16-ounce package marshmallows
4 quarts popped corn
2 cups salted peanuts
1 8-ounce package candy-coated chocolate pieces

Bob Andy Pie

(Old Amish Recipe)

2 **cups sugar**
3½ **tablespoons all-
  purpose flour**
1 **teaspoon cinnamon**
¼ **teaspoon ground
  cloves**
2 **tablespoons butter,
  softened**
3 **eggs, separated**
2 **cups milk**
1 **10-inch deep dish
  pie shell, unbaked**

Combine sugar, flour, cinnamon and cloves. Add butter and mix until crumbly. Add egg yolks and milk, mixing well. Beat egg whites until stiff and fold into yolk mixture. Pour batter into 10-inch pie shell. Bake at 425° for about 15 minutes to brown surface, reduce oven to 350° and bake for about 30 minutes or until done; filling will be soft but not liquid. Yield: 6 to 8 servings.

Perfect Apple Pie

6 **to 8 tart apples,
  peeled and thinly
  sliced**
1 **tablespoon lemon
  juice
  Pastry for double-
  crust 9-inch pie**
2 **tablespoons all-
  purpose flour**
1 **cup sugar
  Dash of salt**
1 **teaspoon cinnamon
  Dash of nutmeg**
2 **tablespoons
  margarine
  Sugar**

Sprinkle apples with lemon juice. Place pastry for 1 crust in 9-inch pie pan. Combine flour, sugar, salt, cinnamon and nutmeg, mixing well. Add dry ingredients to apples, tossing to coat evenly. Pour apples into pastry shell. Dot with margarine. Top with remaining pastry, crimping edges to seal and cutting several slits to vent steam. Sprinkle with sugar. Bake at 400° for 50 minutes or until golden brown. Yield: 6 to 8 servings.

Apple Walnut Upside Down Pie

5 tablespoons butter, melted
½ cup firmly-packed brown sugar
⅓ cup chopped walnuts
Pastry for double-crust 10-inch pie
4 apples, peeled and cut in ¾-inch cubes
1 cup plus 2 tablespoons sugar
3 tablespoons all-purpose flour
¼ teaspoon salt
¾ teaspoon cinnamon
⅛ teaspoon nutmeg

Combine butter and brown sugar, mixing well. Spread mixture in 10-inch pie pan prepared with non-stick vegetable spray. Sprinkle walnuts on sugar layer. Place pastry for 1 crust in pan, being careful to avoid piercing pastry on walnuts. Trim pastry evenly with pan edge. Pour apples into pastry-lined pan. Combine sugar, flour, salt, cinnamon and nutmeg, blending well. Sprinkle dry ingredients on apples. Place remaining pastry on apples. Cut several slits to vent steam. Trim edges, seal and roll toward center of pie; pastry should not touch pan rim. Bake at 375° for 50 to 55 minutes. Use knife tip to loosen edge of pie from pan, invert on serving plate, let stand for 2 minutes and remove pan. Yield: 6 to 8 servings.

Note: Place baking sheet under pie pan to catch bubbling juices during baking.

Buttermilk Pie

1½ cups sugar
½ cup margarine, melted
2 eggs
1½ cups buttermilk
2 teaspoons vanilla or lemon extract
3 tablespoons all-purpose flour
1 unbaked 9-inch pastry shell

Combine sugar, margarine, eggs, buttermilk and vanilla, mixing well. Blend in flour, stirring to remove lumps. Pour filling into pastry shell. Bake at 400° for 20 minutes, reduce oven to 325° and bake for 35 minute or until golden brown. Store in refrigerator but do not freeze. Yield: 6 to 8 servings.

Old Fashioned Butterscotch Pie

2 tablespoons
   margarine
2 cups plus 2
   tablespoons milk,
   divided
1½ cups firmly-packed
   brown sugar
3 tablespoons
   cornstarch
2 eggs, separated
1 teaspoon vanilla
1 baked 9-inch pastry
   shell

Combine margarine, 2 tablespoons milk and brown sugar in skillet. Cook for about 1 minute or until caramelized. Dissolve cornstarch in 2 cups milk. Add yolks and beat well. Stir in vanilla. Add milk liquid to caramelized sugar in skillet. Cook, stirring constantly, until thickened. Pour filling into pastry shell. Prepare meringue, using egg whites, and spread on pie filling. Broil until golden brown. Yield: 6 to 8 servings.

Brownie Pie

1 cup sugar
½ cup butter or
   margarine
2 eggs
1 teaspoon vanilla
½ cup self-rising flour
1 6-ounce package
   chocolate chips
1 cup chopped
   English walnuts
1 unbaked 9-inch
   pastry shell

Cream sugar and butter until smooth. Add eggs and vanilla, beating until blended. Stir in flour, chocolate chips and walnuts. Pour filling into pastry shell. Bake at 350° for 30 minutes or until golden brown. Yield: 6 to 8 servings.

Fudge Meringue Pie

2 cups sugar
3 tablespoons all-purpose flour
3 tablespoons cocoa
2 cups milk
3 eggs, separated
¼ cup butter
1 unbaked 9-inch pastry shell

Combine sugar, flour and cocoa in saucepan. Gradually add milk, blending well. Bring to a boil over medium heat and cook for 1 minute. Beat egg yolks. Add ½ of hot liquid to egg yolks, then add egg yolk mixture to pan liquid. Stir in butter and boil until well thickened. Pour filling into pastry shell. Prepare meringue, using 2 egg whites, and spread on pie filling. Bake at 300° until peaks are golden brown. Yield: 6 to 8 servings.

Chocolate Fudge Pie

1½ cups sugar
2 teaspoons all-purpose flour
3 tablespoons cocoa
½ teaspoon salt
1 13-ounce can evaporated milk
4 egg yolks
2 tablespoons melted butter
2 teaspoons vanilla
1 unbaked 9-inch pastry shell

Sift sugar, flour, cocoa and salt together. Add milk, egg yolks, butter and vanilla, mixing well. Pour filling into pastry shell. Bake at 425° for 20 minutes, reduce oven to 325° and bake for 30 to 35 minutes or until filling is firm. Yield: 6 to 8 servings.

Coconut Pie

2 eggs, lightly beaten
1 cup milk
¼ cup butter, melted
1 cup sugar
3 tablespoons all-
  purpose flour
1 tablespoon vanilla
1 cup moist flaked
  coconut
1 unbaked 9-inch
  pastry shell

Combine eggs, milk and butter. Combine sugar and flour. Add dry ingredients to egg mixture. Stir in vanilla and coconut. Pour filling into pastry shell. Bake at 400° for 10 minutes, reduce oven to 350° and bake for about 30 minutes or until filling is firm and lightly browned. Yield: 6 to 8 servings.

Egg Nog Pie

1¼ cups vanilla wafer
   crumbs
⅓ cup melted butter
1 tablespoon
  unflavored gelatin
¼ cup cold water
¾ cup milk
½ cup sugar
1 tablespoon
  cornstarch
⅛ teaspoon salt
2 egg yolks, beaten
1 tablespoon butter
1 cup whipping
  cream
1 teaspoon vanilla
  Nutmeg

Combine crumbs and melted butter, mixing well. Press crumbs into bottom and on sides of 9-inch pie pan. Dissolve gelatin in water. Combine milk, sugar, cornstarch and salt in saucepan. Cook, stirring constantly, over medium heat until thickened. Add eggs and cook until smooth. Remove from heat. Stir butter and gelatin into custard. Let stand until cool. Whip cream with vanilla. Fold into cooled custard. Pour into pastry shell and sprinkle with nutmeg. Chill before serving. Yield: 6 to 8 servings.

Sour Cream Lemon Pie

1 cup sugar

3 tablespoons cornstarch

¼ cup butter

¼ cup lemon juice

3 egg yolks

1 tablespoon grated lemon peel

1 cup milk

1 cup sour cream

1 baked 9-inch pastry shell

Combine sugar and cornstarch in saucepan. Add butter, lemon juice, egg yolks, lemon peel and milk. Cook over medium heat until thickened. Fold sour cream into filling. Pour into pastry shell. Serve with dollops of whipped cream. Yield: 6 to 8 servings.

Scrivener's Lemon Pie

Pie

1½ cups water

½ cup fresh lemon juice

4 egg yolks

1½ cups sugar

¼ cup cornstarch

Water

1 baked 9-inch pastry shell

Combine water and lemon juice in saucepan. Heat until simmering. Combine egg yolks and sugar, beating well. Add to lemon water and simmer for 2 minutes. Blend cornstarch with enough water to form light paste. Add cornstarch to lemon mixture. Cook, whipping, until thickened. Cool slightly before pouring into pastry shell. Prepare meringue, spread over pie filling to seal at pastry edge. Bake at 350° until meringue is lightly browned. Yield: 6 to 8 servings.

Meringue

4 egg whites

¼ cup sugar

1½ teaspoons cream of tartar

Beat egg whites, sugar and cream of tartar together until stiff. Spread on pie filling.

Grandma Clayton's Coconut Pie

2 cups milk
4 eggs
1 teaspoon vanilla
¾ cup sugar
½ cup biscuit baking
   mix
½ teaspoon butter
1 cup flaked coconut

Combine milk, eggs and vanilla, beating well. Add sugar, baking mix, butter and coconut. Let batter stand for 5 minutes before pouring into buttered 9-inch pie pan. Bake at 375° for 30 minutes. Yield: 6 to 8 servings.

Mississippi Pecan Pie

1 cup sugar
1 cup light corn
   syrup
1 tablespoon butter
1 teaspoon vanilla
3 eggs, well beaten
1 cup broken pecans
1 unbaked 9-inch
   deep dish pastry
   shell

Combine sugar and syrup in saucepan. Bring to a boil and cook for about 5 minutes. Remove from heat and add butter and vanilla, beating well. Very slowly add syrup to eggs, beating constantly. Add pecans. Pour filling into pastry shell. Bake at 350° for about 1 hour and golden brown; pecans will rise to top of filling. Yield: 6 to 8 servings.

Sour Cream Peach Pie

Fresh peaches,
   peeled and sliced
1 unbaked 9-inch
   pastry shell
1 cup sugar
3 tablespoons flour
½ cup sour cream
1 egg

Place peach slices in pastry shell. Combine sugar, flour, sour cream and egg, mixing well. Pour batter over peaches. Bake at 425° for about 45 minutes or until brown crust forms. Yield: 6 to 8 servings.

Maple Nut Chiffon Pie

Pastry

Combine flour and powdered sugar. Cut margarine into dry ingredients to form coarse crumbs. Press mixture into a ball, wrap in wax paper and chill for 30 minutes. Press dough in bottom and on sides of greased 9-inch pie pan, piercing with fork tines in several places. Bake at 400° for 10 minutes. Cool before adding pie filling.

- **1 cup all-purpose flour**
- **2 tablespoons powdered sugar**
- **½ cup margarine**

Filling

Combine gelatin, ½ cup brown sugar and salt in top of double boiler. Beat egg yolks with water and add to gelatin mixture. Cook over simmering water, stirring frequently, for about 5 minutes or until gelatin is dissolved. Remove from heat and stir in maple flavoring. Let stand until room temperature. Beat egg whites until soft peaks form. Gradually add ½ cup brown sugar, beating until stiff, glossy peaks form. Add gelatin mixture and beat for 1 minute. Fold in whipped cream, then pecans. Spread filling in cooled crust. Chill for about 4 hours or until firm. Garnish individual servings with whipped cream and pecan halves. Yield: 6 to 8 servings.

- **1 envelope unflavored gelatin**
- **1 cup firmly-packed light brown sugar, divided**
- **⅛ teaspoon salt**
- **3 eggs, separated**
- **¼ cup water**
- **1¼ teaspoons maple flavoring**
- **1 cup whipping cream, whipped**
- **½ cup chopped pecans**
- **Whipped cream for garnish (optional)**
- **Pecan halves for garnish (optional)**

Hawaiian Pie

1 **15-ounce can crushed pineapple, drained and juice reserved**
Water
3 **tablespoons cornstarch**
½ **cup sugar**
2 **large bananas, sliced**
1⅓ **cups shredded coconut**
½ **cup sliced maraschino cherries**
¼ **to ½ cup chopped pecans**
1 **baked 9-inch pastry shell**
Whipped cream

Add water to reserved pineapple juice to measure 1 cup. Dissolve cornstarch in ½ cup of pineapple water. Combine cornstarch liquid, remaining pineapple water, sugar and pineapple in saucepan. Cook over medium heat, stirring frequently, until thickened. Remove from heat and let stand until cool. Fold bananas, coconut, cherries and pecans into cooled pineapple mixture. Spread fruit filling in pastry shell. Spread whipped cream on filling. Chill until ready to serve. Yield: 6 to 8 servings.

Pumpkin Pie

1 **16-ounce can pumpkin**
¾ **cup sugar**
½ **cup firmly-packed brown sugar**
½ **teaspoon salt**
1½ **teaspoons cinnamon**
½ **teaspoon allspice**
3 **eggs**
1 **13-ounce can evaporated milk**
¼ **cup milk**
½ **teaspoon vanilla**
1 **unbaked 9-inch pastry shell**

Combine pumpkin, sugar, brown sugar, salt, cinnamon and allspice. Add eggs, evaporated milk, milk and vanilla, mixing thoroughly. Pour filling into pastry shell. Bake at 425° for 15 minutes, reduce oven to 350° and bake for 50 minutes. Yield: 6 to 8 servings.

Raisin Cream Pie

1 cup raisins
½ cup water
2 eggs, separated
**2 tablespoons all-
    purpose flour**
¾ cup sugar
¼ teaspoon salt
**2 tablespoons
    margarine**
1 cup milk
½ teaspoon vanilla
**1 baked 9-inch pastry
    shell**

Combine raisins and water in sauce-pan. Cook for 5 minutes, remove from heat and let stand to cool. Beat egg yolks. Combine yolks, flour, sugar, salt, margarine and milk in saucepan. Cook until thickened. Stir in raisins with liquid and vanilla. Pour filling into pastry shell. Prepare meringue, using egg whites. Spread meringue on filling. Broil until lightly browned. Yield: 6 to 8 servings.

Strawberry Cream Pie

¼ cup sugar
**1 8-ounce package
    cream cheese,
    softened**
**½ teaspoon vanilla
    Dash of nutmeg**
**1 cup sliced
    strawberries,
    divided**
**1 cup whipping
    cream**
¼ cup powdered sugar
**1 9-inch graham
    cracker crust**

Combine sugar, cream cheese, vanilla and nutmeg, mixing until well blended. Mash ¾ cup strawberries and add to creamed mixture. Whip cream with powdered sugar until stiff peaks form. Fold whipped cream into straw-berry mixture. Spread filling in crust. Chill for several hours or overnight. Garnish with reserved strawberry slices. Yield: 6 to 8 servings.

Never Fail Pie Crust

½ **cup vegetable shortening**
1 **cup all-purpose flour**
⅓ **cup milk**
All-purpose flour

Using pastry blender, cut shortening into flour until well mixed. Stir in milk. Pastry will appear very moist. Dust palms with flour to handle pastry. Roll pastry on floured surface to circle to fit pie pan. Place in pan, add filling and crimp pastry edges. Bake according to pie recipe. Yield: 6 to 8 servings.

Apricot Delight

1 **3-ounce package apricot gelatin**
1 **cup boiling water**
1 **cup cold water**
1 **15-ounce can crushed pineapple, drained and juice reserved**
3 **large bananas, sliced**
1 **10-ounce package miniature marshmallows**
1 **cup sugar**
¼ **cup all-purpose flour**
2 **tablespoons butter**
2 **eggs, beaten**
2 **3-ounce packages cream cheese, softened**
1 **8-ounce container frozen whipped topping, thawed**
1 **cup chopped pecans**

Dissolve gelatin in boiling water. Add cold water and chill for 30 minutes or until consistency of egg white. Fold pineapple into gelatin. Pour mixture into serving dish. Place banana slices and marshmallows on gelatin mixture. Combine 1 cup pineapple juice, sugar, flour, butter and eggs in saucepan. Cook over medium heat, stirring constantly, until pudding consistency. Add cream cheese and stir until partially melted. Pour pudding on marshmallow layer. Combine whipped topping and pecans and spread on pudding layer. Chill for at least 3 hours. Yield: 12 servings.

Apple Dumplings

Combine sugar, water, cinnamon and nutmeg in saucepan. Simmer until syrup consistency. Stir in butter and set aside. Sift flour, baking powder and salt together. Cut shortening into dry ingredients. Add milk and stir until moistened. Roll dough to ¼-inch thickness on floured surface. Cut into six 5-inch squares. Place 4 apple quarters on each square, sprinkle generously with additional sugar, cinnamon and nutmeg and dot with butter. Fold corners to center and pinch to seal. Place dumplings 1 inch apart in greased baking pan. Pour syrup over dumplings. Bake at 375° for 35 minutes. Serve hot with cream. Yield: 6 servings.

- 2 cups sugar
- 2 cups water
- ¼ teaspoon cinnamon
- ¼ teaspoon nutmeg
- ¼ cup butter
- 2 cups all-purpose flour
- 2 teaspoons baking powder
- 1 teaspoon salt
- ¾ cup vegetable shortening
- ½ cup milk
- 6 apples, peeled and quartered
- Sugar
- Cinnamon
- Nutmeg
- Butter

Fresh Blueberry Cobbler

Combine blueberries, water and sugar in saucepan. Bring to a boil, reduce heat and simmer for 2 minutes, stirring constantly. Pour blueberry mixture into 8x8x2-inch baking dish. Combine flour, brown sugar, baking powder, salt and nutmeg. Cut margarine into dry ingredients until consistency of coarse meal. Sprinkle crumbs on blueberry mixture. Bake at 350° for 25 minutes. Yield: 9 servings.

- 2 cups fresh blueberries
- ¼ cup water
- ⅔ cup sugar
- 1 cup all-purpose flour
- ½ cup firmly-packed brown sugar
- ½ teaspoon baking powder
- Pinch of salt
- Pinch of nutmeg
- ⅓ cup margarine

Blueberry Peach Cobbler

½ **cup butter or margarine**
1 **cup all-purpose flour**
1¼ **cups sugar, divided**
2 **teaspoons baking powder**
½ **cup milk**
2 **cups sliced fresh peaches**
2 **cups fresh blueberries**

Melt butter in 2½-quart casserole. Combine flour, ¾ cup sugar and baking powder. Add milk and blend thoroughly. Pour batter into melted butter in casserole; do not stir. Combine peaches, blueberries and ½ cup sugar. Spoon fruit on batter; do not stir. Bake at 350° for 45 to 55 minutes. Yield: 6 to 8 servings.

Blueberry Supreme

1 **cup all-purpose flour**
¼ **cup firmly-packed brown sugar**
½ **cup butter**
1 **cup chopped nuts**
1 **12-ounce carton frozen whipped topping, thawed, divided**
1 **8-ounce package cream cheese, softened**
¾ **cup sugar**
1 **teaspoon vanilla**
1 **21-ounce can blueberry pie filling**

Combine flour, brown sugar, butter and nuts, mixing well. Lightly press mixture into 9x5x3-inch loaf pan. Bake at 350° for 20 minutes. Let stand until cool. Combine ½ of whipped topping, cream cheese, sugar and vanilla. Spread filling on crust. Spoon pie filling on creme layer and top with remaining whipped topping. Chill. Yield: 8 to 10 servings.

Lu's Favorite Pudding

Combine evaporated milk, condensed milk and pudding mix. Add ⅔ of whipped topping to pudding mixture. Layer wafers, bananas and pudding in serving dish. Spread remaining topping on pudding layer. Chill. Yield: 8 servings.

- **1 14-ounce can evaporated milk**
- **1 7-ounce can sweetened condensed milk**
- **1 3¾-ounce package French vanilla instant pudding mix**
- **1 12-ounce carton frozen whipped topping, thawed, divided**
- **½ 12-ounce package vanilla wafers**
- **2 or 3 ripe bananas, sliced**

Brownie Pudding

Sift flour, sugar, 2 tablespoons cocoa, baking powder and salt together. Add milk, vanilla and shortening, mixing until smooth. Stir in walnuts. Pour batter into greased 8x8x2-inch baking dish. Combine brown sugar and ¼ cup cocoa. Sprinkle on batter. Pour hot water on batter; do not mix. Bake at 350° for 40 to 45 minutes. Serve with whipped cream. Yield: 6 to 9 servings.

- **1 cup all-purpose flour**
- **¾ cup sugar**
- **¼ cup plus 2 tablespoons cocoa, divided**
- **2 teaspoons baking powder**
- **½ teaspoon salt**
- **½ cup milk**
- **1 teaspoon vanilla**
- **2 tablespoons vegetable shortening, melted**
- **¾ cup walnuts**
- **¾ cup firmly-packed brown sugar**
- **1¾ cups hot water**

Butterscotch Delight

1 cup all-purpose
  flour
½ cup chopped pecans
½ cup margarine,
  melted
1 8-ounce package
  cream cheese,
  softened
1 cup powdered sugar
1 12-ounce carton
  frozen whipped
  topping, thawed,
  divided
2 3¾-ounce packages
  butterscotch
  instant pudding
  mix
3 cups milk
  Chopped pecans

Combine flour, pecans and margarine, mixing well. Press mixture into bottom of 13x9x2-inch baking dish. Bake at 350° for 15 minutes. Let stand until cool. Combine cream cheese and powdered sugar, creaming until smooth. Fold 1 cup whipped topping into creamed mixture. Spread on cooled crust. Combine pudding and milk, beating well. Pour pudding on creme layer. Spread remaining topping on pudding layer and sprinkle with pecans. Chill. Yield: 12 to 16 servings.

Skillet Custard

2 eggs, beaten
¼ cup sugar
⅛ teaspoon salt
½ teaspoon vanilla
1½ cups milk

Combine eggs, sugar, salt, vanilla and milk, stirring until sugar is dissolved. Pour into 4 buttered custard cups. Place cups in skillet and add water to level of custard in cups. Cover and bring to a boil. Turn heat off and let stand for 10 minutes before removing from skillet. Yield: 4 servings.

Something Chocolate

Cut butter into flour, blending well.
Press mixture into bottom of 13x9x2-
inch baking dish. Bake at 350° for 10
to 15 minutes. Let stand until cool.
Combine cream cheese, powdered
sugar and whipped topping. Spread on
cooled crust. Combine pudding and
milk, beating well. Spread pudding on
creme layer. Spread additional topping
on pudding layer and sprinkle with
pecans. Chill. Yield: 12 to 16 servings.

½ **cup butter or margarine**
1 **cup all-purpose flour**
1 **8-ounce package cream cheese, softened**
1 **cup powdered sugar**
1½ **cups frozen whipped topping, thawed**
1 **6-ounce package chocolate instant pudding mix**
2¾ **cups milk**
1 **cup broken pecans (optional)**
Whipped topping

D's Strawberry Delight

Dissolve gelatin in boiling water. Add
strawberries, bananas and pineapple.
Pour ½ of fruit mixture into 13x9x2-
inch baking dish. Chill until firm.
Combine sour cream and sugar.
Spread sour cream on chilled fruit
layer. Pour remaining fruit mixture on
sour cream layer. Chill until firm.
Serve plain or with whipped topping.
Yield: 12 to 16 servings.

2 **3-ounce packages strawberry gelatin**
1 **cup boiling water**
1 **10-ounce package frozen strawberries, thawed**
3 **bananas, mashed**
1 **8-ounce can crushed pineapple**
1 **cup sour cream**
1 **teaspoon sugar**

Peanut Butter Delight Cake

Cake

- 2¾ **cups all-purpose flour**
- 2 **teaspoons baking powder**
- 1 **teaspoon baking soda**
- ½ **teaspoon salt**
- 1 **cup sugar**
- ½ **cup firmly-packed brown sugar**
- ¾ **cup butter-flavor shortening**
- ¾ **cup creamy peanut butter**
- 3 **large eggs**
- 1½ **teaspoons vanilla extract**
- 1 **cup buttermilk**
- ¾ **cup chocolate syrup**

Preheat oven to 350°. Spray Bundt pan with non-stick cooking spray. Sift flour with baking soda and salt. Combine sugar, brown sugar, butter-flavor shortening and peanut butter in a large bowl. Beat with mixer at low speed until creamy. Beat in eggs, one at a time. Add vanilla; mix well. Add dry ingredients alternately with buttermilk, beating at low speed after each addition until mixed. Spoon 2 cups peanut butter batter into medium bowl. Stir in chocolate syrup. Spoon the remaining peanut butter batter into Bundt pan. Spoon the chocolate batter over the peanut butter batter. Do not mix. Bake one hour and 10 minutes to one hour and 20 minutes, or until toothpick inserted in center comes out clean. Cool 45 minutes before removing from pan. Place fluted side up on serving plate, cool completely.

Glaze

- 1 **cup confectioners sugar**
- ¼ **cup chocolate syrup**
- 1 **teaspoon vanilla extract**
- ¼ **cup chopped salted peanuts**

For glaze, combine sugar, syrup and vanilla in a small bowl. Stir to blend. Add water one drop at a time until desired consistency. Spread glaze over top of cooled cake, allowing glaze to drip down sides. Sprinkle with peanuts.

Mexican Flan

**4 cups milk,
constituted from
non-fat dry milk
powder**
1 cup sugar, divided
**1¼ cups egg substitute
Dash of salt**
**1 teaspoon vanilla
Water**
2 tablespoons water

Pour milk into saucepan. Cook over medium heat until near boil; remove before milk boils. Cool by placing pan in cold water. Combine ½ cup sugar, egg substitute, salt and vanilla, mixing well. Place 8 custard cups in baking pan. Combine ½ cup sugar and 2 tablespoons water in small stainless steel saucepan. Cook, stirring, until sugar turns is caramel. Spoon 1 teaspoon caramel into each custard cup, then distribute remaining caramel evenly among cups. Add milk to egg mixture. Distribute liquid evenly among cups, filling to top of each. Place pan on top shelf of oven pre-heated to 325°. Add water to 1-inch depth in pan. Cover cups with alumi-num foil sheet. Bake for 1 to 1½ hours or until knife tip inserted in center of custard cup comes out clean. Let stand until cool. Cover with plastic wrap and store in refrigerator. Use knife tip to loosen custard from edge of cups and invert on serving dishes. Yield: 8 servings.

Note: Dessert contains no cholesterol or fat.

Rhubarb Dessert

Crust

1 cup all-purpose
  flour
¼ cup plus 1
  tablespoon
  powdered sugar
½ cup butter

*Combine flour and powdered sugar.
Add butter and mix thoroughly. Press
mixture in bottom of 8x8x2-inch
baking pan. Bake at 350° for 15
minutes.*

Filling

¼ cup all-purpose
  flour
1½ cups sugar
¾ teaspoon baking
  powder
2 eggs
2 cups sliced rhubarb

*Combine flour, sugar and baking
powder. Add eggs and rhubarb. Pour
fruit mixture on partially baked crust.
Bake for 45 minutes. Yield: 6 to 9
servings.*

Fruit Pizza

Crust

¾ cup butter, softened
½ cup powdered sugar
1½ cups all-purpose
  flour

*Cream butter and sugar together until
fluffy. Blend in flour. Press dough
evenly on pizza pan. Bake at 300° for
20 to 25 minutes. Let stand until cool.*

Filling

Sliced kiwi,
  bananas,
  nectarines, peaches,
  strawberries or
  other fruit
¼ cup sugar
1 tablespoon
  cornstarch
½ cup pineapple juice
½ teaspoon lemon
  juice

*Arrange fruit on cooled crust. Combine
sugar and cornstarch in small saucepan. Add pineapple and lemon juices.
Cook over medium heat, stirring
constantly, until thickened. Let stand
until cool. Pour glaze over fruit. Chill
before serving. Yield: 10 to 12 servings.*

Melt margarine in 2-quart casserole.
Combine flour, sugar and baking
powder. Add milk, mixing well. Pour
batter on butter in casserole. Spoon
fruit with juice on batter. Bake at 400°
for 30 minutes or until golden brown.
Yield: 5 or 6 servings.

Easy Fruit Cobbler

- ½ **cup margarine**
- 1 **cup all-purpose flour**
- 1 **cup sugar**
- 1⅓ **tablespoons baking powder**
- 1 **cup milk**
- 1 **28-ounce can fruit, undrained**

Prepare 13x9x2-inch baking pan with
non-stick vegetable spray. Dissolve 2
envelopes unflavored gelatin in 2 cups
boiling water. Add milk and set aside.
Dissolve ½ envelope unflavored gelatin
and 1 package flavored gelatin in 1
cup boiling water. Pour into prepared
pan. Freeze for 15 minutes or until
firm; do not over freeze. Pour 1 cup
milk mixture on frozen layer. Freeze
for 15 minutes. Repeat layers 3 times.
Cut frozen layers into squares to serve.
Yield: 16 servings.

Gelatin Squares

- 4 **envelopes unflavored gelatin, divided**
- 6 **cups boiling water**
- 1 **14-ounce can sweetened condensed milk**
- 4 **3-ounce packages flavored gelatin**

Combine orange drink, milk and
pineapple. Pour into canister of ice
cream freezer. Freeze according to
freezer directions. Yield: 16 servings.

Variation: Strawberry or peach drink
may be substituted for orange and
crushed strawberries or peaches used
instead of pineapple.

Sherbet

- 5 **12-ounce cans orange carbonated drink**
- 2 **14-ounce cans sweetened condensed milk**
- 1 **cup crushed pineapple**

Pumpkin Ice Cream Pie

1 pint vanilla ice
   cream, softened
1 baked 9-inch pastry
   shell
1½ cups sugar
½ teaspoon salt
1 teaspoon cinnamon
½ teaspoon ginger
1 teaspoon vanilla
1 16-ounce can
   pumpkin
1½ cups whipping
   cream, divided
½ cup slivered
   almonds, toasted

Spread ice cream in pastry. Place in freezer while preparing pumpkin filling. Combine sugar, salt, cinnamon and ginger. Add vanilla and pumpkin, blending well. Whip 1 cup cream until stiff, fold into pumpkin mixture and spread on ice cream in pastry shell. Freeze, uncovered, until firm. Cover with aluminum foil and freeze for 6 to 8 hours or overnight and firm. Whip ½ cup cream until stiff, spoon dollops around edge of pie and sprinkle with almonds. Yield: 8 servings.

Ice Cream Crunch Cake

1 12-ounce package
   chocolate chips
⅔ cup smooth peanut
   butter
6 cups crispy rice
   cereal
1 gallon vanilla ice
   cream, softened
   Whipped cream
   (optional)
   Strawberries
   (optional)

Combine chocolate chips and peanut butter in saucepan. Cook over low heat, stirring several times, until chips are melted and blended. Add cereal, mixing to coat well. Spread cereal mixture on baking sheet and let stand until cool. Break into small pieces. Reserving 1 cup cereal mixture, combine remainder with ice cream. Press ice cream into 10-inch springform pan. Press reserved cereal on top. Freeze until firm. To serve, remove pan sides and garnish with whipped cream and strawberries. Yield: 16 to 20 servings.

NEW EVERY MORNING

Because of the Lord's great love we are not consumed, for His compassions never fail. They are new every morning; great is thy faithfulness.

LAMENTATIONS 3: 22,23

BREAKFAST & BRUNCH

Sausage Casserole

8 slices day-old
   bread, crusts
   trimmed and cubed
2 pounds bulk pork
   sausage, cooked,
   crumbled and
   drained
1½ cups (6 ounces)
   grated sharp cheese
6 eggs, lightly beaten
2½ to 3 cups milk
1 tablespoon minced
   onion
1 tablespoon brown
   sugar
¼ teaspoon salt
⅛ teaspoon black
   pepper
¼ teaspoon paprika
¼ teaspoon dry
   mustard
⅛ teaspoon red pepper
   (optional)

Layer, in order listed, bread cubes, sausage and cheese in greased 2-quart casserole. Combine eggs, milk, onion, brown sugar, salt, black pepper, paprika, mustard and red pepper. Pour egg mixture over cheese layer. Chill, covered, overnight. Remove from refrigerator and let stand, uncovered, for 1 hour before baking. Bake at 350° for 45 minutes to 1 hour. Yield: 16 to 20 servings.

Note: To lower cholesterol and fat content of casserole, drain sausage in colander and rinse with hot water to remove excess fat. Substitute fat-free cheese for regular cheese, use egg substitute instead of eggs and use ½% milk instead of whole milk.

Breakfast Casserole

Butter 8 slices bread and place, buttered side down, in 13x9x2-inch baking pan or dish. Sprinkle cheese and ham on bread slices. Arrange 8 slices unbuttered bread on ham layer. Combine eggs, milk, salt and mustard. Pour egg mixture over bread. Chill, covered, overnight. Remove from refrigerator 1 hour before baking. Pour melted butter on bread layer and sprinkle with corn flakes. Bake at 350° for 1 hour. Yield: 16 to 20 servings.

16 slices bread, crusts trimmed
   Butter, softened
2 cups (8 ounces) grated Cheddar cheese
2 cups diced ham
6 eggs, beaten
3 cups milk
½ teaspoon salt
1 teaspoon dry mustard
¼ cup melted butter
1 cup corn flakes

Myrtle's Coffee Cake

Mixing with hands, combine flour, brown sugar and margarine. Spoon 1½ cups of mixture into greased 8x8x2-inch baking pan. Add egg, baking soda, cinnamon and sour cream to remaining flour mixture, blending thoroughly. Pour batter into pan. Bake at 375° for 40 minutes. Yield: 9 servings.

2 cups all-purpose flour
2 cups firmly-packed brown sugar
½ cup margarine, at room temperature
1 egg
1 teaspoon baking soda
1 teaspoon cinnamon or nutmeg
1 cup sour cream or buttermilk

Pineapple Coffee Cake

Filling

- ½ **cup sugar**
- 3 **tablespoons cornstarch**
- ¼ **teaspoon salt**
- 1 **egg yolk, lightly beaten**
- 1 **15-ounce can crushed pineapple**

Combine sugar, cornstarch, salt, egg and pineapple in saucepan. Cook over medium heat, stirring frequently, until thickened. Let stand until cool.

Crust

- 4 **cups all-purpose flour**
- 1 **tablespoon sugar**
- 1 **cup butter**
- 1 **envelope dry active yeast**
- ¼ **cup warm (110° to 115°) water**
- ⅔ **cup milk, scalded and cooled**
- 4 **egg yolks, lightly beaten**

Combine flour, sugar and butter, blending until consistency of coarse crumbs. Dissolve yeast in warm water. Add yeast liquid, milk and egg yolks to crumbs, mixing well. Shape dough into a ball and divide in 2 portions. Roll ½ of dough to rectangle shape on baking sheet. Spread pineapple filling on dough. Roll remaining dough into rectangle and cut into strips. Place in lattice design on pineapple filling. Let rise for 1 hour. Bake at 350° for 40 minutes. Yield: 16 to 20 servings.

Easy Apple Coffee Cake

Combine pie filling and eggs. Add cake mix and beat well. Pour batter into greased 13x9x2-inch baking pan. Bake at 350° for 35 minutes. Combine brown sugar, flour, cinnamon and walnuts. Sprinkle mixture on warm cake. Yield: 16 to 20 servings.

1 21-ounce can apple pie filling
3 eggs
1 18½-ounce package yellow cake mix
½ cup firmly-packed brown sugar
1 tablespoon all-purpose flour
1 teaspoon cinnamon
½ cup chopped walnuts

Peach Pancake Bake

Pancake

Combine pancake or biscuit mix, milk, shortening and eggs, mixing well. Pour batter into greased 13x9x2-inch baking pan. Arrange peach slices on batter. Sprinkle with brown sugar and cinnamon. Bake at 350° for 30 to 35 minutes. Prepare filling and serve on baked pancake. Yield: 8 to 12 servings.

2 cups pancake or biscuit baking mix
1 cup milk
1 tablespoon melted shortening
2 eggs
2 16-ounce cans sliced peaches, drained and juice reserved
Brown sugar
Cinnamon

Filling

Combine peach juice, adding water if necessary to measure 2 cups, syrup and butter in saucepan. Add small amount of cornstarch to thicken. Simmer until thickened and warm.

2 cups peach juice
1 cup maple syrup
2 tablespoons butter or margarine
Cornstarch

Fluffy Sour Cream Pancakes

3 tablespoons melted
  margarine
3 eggs
1½ cups sour cream
2 tablespoons sugar
1 teaspoon baking
  powder
1 teaspoon baking
  soda
½ teaspoon salt
2 cups all-purpose
  flour
1 to 2 cups milk

Combine margarine, eggs, sour cream, sugar, baking powder, baking soda and salt, mixing well. Alternately add flour and milk until consistency of pancake batter. Ladle batter, ¼ to ⅓ cup for each pancake, onto hot greased griddle and cook until done, turning once. Yield: 4 or 5 servings.

Old Fashioned Oatmeal Pancakes

2 cups uncooked
  regular oats
2½ cups buttermilk
1 cup all-purpose
  flour
1 tablespoon sugar
1 teaspoon baking
  soda
1 teaspoon salt
¼ cup melted butter
  or margarine

Combine oats and buttermilk. Chill overnight. Add flour, sugar, baking soda, salt and butter to oat mixture, adding additional buttermilk if batter is too thick. Ladle batter, ¼ to ⅓ cup for each pancake, onto hot greased griddle and cook until done, turning once. Yield: 4 to 6 servings.

Cornmeal Pancakes

Combine cornmeal, sugar and salt. Gradually add boiling water, stirring to blend. Let stand, covered, for 10 minutes. Beat egg, milk and butter together. Add to cornmeal mixture. Sift flour and baking powder together. Add dry ingredients to cornmeal mixture, stirring just until moistened. Ladle batter, ¼ to ⅓ cup for each pancake, onto hot greased griddle and cook until done, turning once. Yield: 3 or 4 servings.

1 cup cornmeal
1 to 2 tablespoons sugar
1 teaspoon salt
1 cup boiling water
1 egg
½ cup milk
2 tablespoons melted butter
½ cup bread flour, sifted
2 teaspoons baking powder

NOT BY BREAD ALONE

Honey Coconut Toast

2 **eggs, beaten**
2 **tablespoons buttermilk**
½ **teaspoon vanilla extract**
⅛ **teaspoon ground cinnamon**
2 **sliced raisin bread**
2 **teaspoons margarine**
1 **teaspoon honey, heated**
2 **teaspoons shredded coconut**

In shallow bowl combine eggs with buttermilk, vanilla and cinnamon. Dip bread into egg mixture, turning on both sides. Let stand until most of the liquid is absorbed. Heat margarine in non-stick skillet and add bread; pour any remaining egg mixture over bread. Cook, turning to brown both sides. Transfer to nonstick baking sheet; spread each slice with ½ teaspoon honey and sprinkle each with 1 teaspoon coconut. Broil 5 minutes. Serve immediately.

Note: Ingredient amounts are for 2 slices of bread. If you would like to increase portions, you may double or triple the ingredient amounts.

CELEBRATION

Bring the fatted calf and kill it.
Let's have a feast and celebrate
For this son of mine was dead
and is alive again;
he was lost and is found.

LUKE 15.23,24

H O L I D A Y   F E A S T

Cranberry Glazed Turkey Patties

1 pound ground
turkey
1 cup finely crushed
round buttery
crackers
2 teaspoons minced
onion flakes
½ cup egg substitute
3 tablespoons canola
oil
1 16-ounce can whole
cranberry sauce
½ cup water
1 teaspoon chicken
bouillon granules
1 tablespoon dry
white wine

Combine turkey, cracker crumbs, onion and egg substitute, mixing well. Shape mixture into 6 to 8 patties. Sauté well in oil in skillet, turning to brown on both sides. Remove patties from skillet. Combine cranberry sauce, water, bouillon and wine in skillet. Cook to reduce liquid slightly, then add patties to sauce. Simmer, covered, for 20 to 30 minutes. Spoon sauce over individual patties to serve. If sauce is too thick, thin with small amount of water. Yield: 6 to 8 servings.

Ollie Bollen

(Dutch New Year's
Treat)

6½ cups all-purpose
flour
½ cup sugar
1 teaspoon salt
2 envelopes dry active
yeast
4 cups warm milk
2 cups raisins
4 eggs, beaten
Vegetable oil for
deep frying

Combine flour, sugar, salt and yeast. Add milk, raisins and eggs, beating well with wooden spoon. Let batter rise 1 to 2 hours and bubbling ceases. Drop tablespoonfuls of batter into oil heated to 350 to 375°, deep frying until golden brown, and drain on paper towel. Yield: 6 to 7 dozen.

Cranberry Casserole

Combine cranberries and apples. Add sugar and toss to coat thoroughly. Spoon fruit into 11x7x1½-inch baking dish. Combine margarine, oats, flour, brown sugar and pecans. Sprinkle crumb mixture on fruit. Bake at 350° for 1 hour. Yield: 6 to 8 servings.

- 2 cups fresh cranberries
- 3 cups sliced or chopped apples
- 1¼ cups sugar
- ½ cup margarine, melted
- 1½ cups uncooked quick-cooking oats
- ⅓ cup all-purpose flour
- ½ cup firmly-packed brown sugar
- ½ cup chopped pecans

Orange Sweet Potato Casserole

Mash sweet potatoes until smooth and fluffy. Add butter, brown sugar, salt, orange juice, orange peel and vanilla, beating until blended. Spread mixture in buttered 2-quart casserole. Bake at 350° for 30 minutes. Sprinkle marshmallows on sweet potato mixture and continue baking for about 10 minutes or until marshmallows are golden brown. Yield: 6 to 8 servings.

- 8 medium-sized sweet potatoes or yams, cooked and peeled
- ½ cup butter or margarine
- ⅓ cup firmly-packed brown sugar
- ½ teaspoon salt
- ½ cup orange juice
  Grated peel of 1 orange
- ½ teaspoon vanilla
- 2 cups miniature marshmallows

Holiday Sweet Potato Soufflé

4 **cups cooked and mashed sweet potatoes**
2 **cups sugar**
3 **eggs**
½ **cup margarine, softened**
1 **tablespoon vanilla**
¼ **cup milk**
¾ **cup firmly-packed brown sugar**
½ **cup all-purpose flour**
½ **cup margarine**
1 **cup chopped nuts**

Combine sweet potatoes, sugar, eggs, softened margarine, vanilla and milk, beating until smooth. Spread mixture in well-greased 9x9x2-inch baking pan or dish. Combine brown sugar, flour, margarine and nuts, mixing until crumb consistency. Sprinkle nut mixture on sweet potato mixture. Bake at 350° for 40 minutes. Let stand for 10 minutes before serving. Yield: 6 to 8 servings.

Apple Cranberry Pie

½ **cup sugar**
¾ **cup firmly-packed brown sugar**
⅓ **cup all-purpose flour**
1 **teaspoon cinnamon**
4 **cups peeled, sliced sweet apples**
2 **cups fresh or frozen whole cranberries**
  Pastry for double-crust 9-inch pie
2 **tablespoons butter or margarine**

Combine sugar, brown sugar, flour and cinnamon. Add apples and cranberries, tossing to coat thoroughly. Spread fruit in pastry-lined pie pan. Dot with butter. Top with remaining pastry, crimping edges to seal and cutting several slits in pastry to vent steam. Bake at 325° for 40 minutes or until crust is golden brown. Yield: 6 to 8 servings.

Holiday Honey Cake

Combine egg yolks and sugar, beating well. Add honey, oil and vanilla, mixing thoroughly. Sift flour, allspice, cinnamon and nutmeg together. Dissolve baking soda in coffee. Alternately add 2 cups spiced flour and coffee liquid to honey mixture. Mix remaining spiced flour with lemon peel, raisins, apple and nuts. Add fruit mixture to batter. Beat egg whites with salt until stiff. Fold egg whites into batter. Spread batter in wax paper-lined 14x10x2-inch baking pan. Bake at 350° for 1 hour and 10 minutes. Cool in pan for 15 minutes. Yield: 20 servings.

5 eggs, separated
1 cup sugar
1 cup honey
1 cup vegetable oil
2 teaspoons vanilla
4 cups all-purpose flour, sifted 3 times
1 teaspoon allspice
1 teaspoon cinnamon
½ teaspoon nutmeg
1 tablespoon baking soda
1½ cups lukewarm coffee
Grated peel of ½ lemon
¾ cup raisins
1 apple, unpeeled, grated
¾ cup chopped nuts
Dash of salt

Christmas Cookies

1 cup firmly-packed brown sugar
½ cup butter, softened
4 eggs, well beaten
3 tablespoons brandy
1 teaspoon vanilla
½ teaspoon nutmeg
3 cups all-purpose flour, divided
1 teaspoon baking soda
1 16-ounce package golden raisins
1 16-ounce package candied cherries, chopped
1 8-ounce package candied pineapple, chopped
1 pound chopped pecans

Cream brown sugar and butter together until smooth. Add eggs, brandy, vanilla and nutmeg, beating well. Sift 2½ cups flour and baking soda together. Add dry ingredients to creamed mixture. Mix ½ cup flour, raisins, cherries, pineapple and pecans together. Add fruit mixture to dough. Drop dough by teaspoonfuls on greased baking sheet. Bake at 350° for 20 minutes. Yield: 9 to 10 dozen.

Sugar Plum Loaf

Cream sugar, shortening and eggs together until light and fluffy. Add buttermilk, lemon juice and orange extract. Combine coconut, dates, candy and pecans. Sift flour, baking soda and salt together. Add dry ingredients to fruit mixture, tossing to coat well. Add fruit mixture to creamed mixture. Spread batter in 2 wax paper-lined 9x5x3-inch loaf pans. Bake at 300° for 1 hour and 50 minutes or until wooden pick inserted near center comes out clean. Cool in pan for 5 minutes. Remove from pans and using wooden pick, punch holes in top of loaves. Drizzle glaze over loaves. Wrap tightly in aluminum foil. Loaves may be frozen. Yield: 20 to 24 servings.

Combine powdered sugar, juice and extract, blending until smooth. Drizzle glaze over warm loaves.

Cake

- 1¾ cups sugar
- ¾ cup vegetable shortening
- 4 eggs
- ¾ cup buttermilk
- 1 tablespoon lemon juice
- 1 teaspoon orange extract
- 1 3½-ounce can flaked coconut
- 1 8-ounce package chopped dates
- 1 cup chopped orange slice candy
- 1½ cups chopped pecans
- 4 cups all-purpose flour
- 1 teaspoon baking soda
- Dash of salt

Glaze

- 1 cup powdered sugar
- 2 to 3 tablespoons orange juice
- ½ teaspoon orange extract

Contributors

Mrs. George Akkerman • San Antonio, Texas

Carol Anderson • San Antonio, Texas

Kathleen Anders • San Antonio, Texas

Katheryn Arriba • San Antonio, Texas

Judy Ashmore • Richfield, Minnesota

Corenia Arguelles • San Antonio, Texas

Lynn Arvin • San Antonio, Texas

Natalie Arvin • San Antonio, Texas

Tom Bailey • Blanco, Texas

Virginia Bailey • Blanco, Texas

Blanche Ball • San Antonio, Texas

Brenda Barabez • San Antonio, Texas

Sheila Barge • Zavalla, Texas

Carole Barker • Fort Wayne, Indiana

Frances Barnes • Salem, Oregon

Viola Barrass • Warren, Ohio

Marjorie Beasley • Birmingham, Alabama

Pat Beauchamp • Edmonds, Washington

Keith Becker • San Antonio, Texas

Jennelle Bedford • San Antonio, Texas

Lisa Benoit • San Antonio, Texas

Menta Bickle • San Antonio, Texas

Anna Bis-Bing • Hanover, Pennsylvania

Helen Bish • Butler, Pennsylvania

Sue Blair • San Antonio, Texas

Mrs. Donald Blake • South Point, Ohio

Joe Blanchard • San Antonio, Texas

Janice Blosser • Lincoln, Nebraska

Marcia Boggs • San Antonio, Texas

Lee Boozer • Oxford, Alabama

Lola Bottoms • Midwest City, Oklahoma

Hulene Bowden • Owasso, Oklahoma

Anna Brazell • Desdemona, Texas

Billie Brooke • Bisalia, California

Leola Brower • Liberty, North Carolina

Floreine Burbick • Butler, Ohio

Laura Burke • Dearborn Heights, Michigan

Alice Campbell • Indianapolis, Indiana

Marie Capps • Ottawa, Illinois

Pat Carberry • San Antonio, Texas

Maria Carol • San Antonio, Texas

Brenda Castro • San Antonio, Texas

Ruth Carlson • Webster, Texas

Mrs. Charles Carlton • Little River, South Carolina

Terri Carrico • San Antonio, Texas

Shirley Cates • San Antonio, Texas

Kathleen Clark • San Antonio, Texas

Bonnie Crisp • Banner, Kentucky

David and Carolyn Crump • Mineola, Texas

Dorenda Curry • San Antonio, Texas

Laverne Davis • Rosenberg, Texas

Patti De La Garza • San Antonio, Texas

Grace De Rosso • Clearwater, Florida

Celena Dennis • Orinda, California

Mary C. Dietrich • Varna, Illinois

Maggie Dietz • San Antonio, Texas

Betty Dixon • Colorado Springs, Colorado

Orvaleta Dodd • Raymond, Washington

Sabrina Dodson • Von Ormy, Texas

Effie M. Dunagan • Blythe, California

Beatrice Dye • Yuba City, California

Beverley Ellis • San Antonio, Texas

Mary Eilert • San Antonio, Texas

V. W. Eilert • San Antonio, Texas

Linda Evans • Rocky Mount, North Carolina

Janet Fenner • Warren, Michigan

Lillie Fetherlin • Cedar Park, Texas

Sandy Farhart • San Antonio, Texas

Odessa Flack • San Antonio, Texas

Betty A. Flexsenhar • Dekin, Illinois

Heather Fitzgerald • San Antonio, Texas

Betty French • Lithia, Florida

Bob and Ruth Friedrichs • Fair Oaks Ranch, Texas

Pastor and Christine Frueh • Seffner, Florida

Pat Galloway • San Antonio, Texas

Robert Garay • Benton, Arkansas

George Garrett • Menlo Park, California

Martha Garvey • Chandon, Ohio

Mary Gavalis • Winter Haven, Florida

Helen Gehron • Fort Wayne, Indiana

Louise Gilbert • Kendall, Florida

Arthur Glowka • San Antonio, Texas

Pat Gordon • Oakdale, Louisiana

Carlene Gray • Benton, Arkansas

Lestra Gross • San Antonio, Texas

Loretta and George Grunewald •
   Shenandoah, Virginia

Tina Guajardo • San Antonio, Texas

Ann Habenicht • San Antonio, Texas

Joan Haggard • Vincennes, Indiana

Joy Haney • Forest City, North Carolina

Amy Hariston • Boerne, Texas

Janice Hariston • Boerne, Texas

Faye Harris • Destin, Florida

Katherine Harris • San Antonio, Texas

Della Harrison • Lexington, Kentucky

Pat Hartha • Balto, Maryland

Carol Hartwell • Magnolia, California

Linda Harvey • San Antonio, Texas

Connie Herrejon • San Antonio, Texas

Jimmie Hill • San Antonio, Texas

Missy Hlavaty • San Antonio, Texas

Mary Hoch • San Antonio, Texas

Mildred Hogan • San Antonio, Texas

Carol Hockenbury • Alliance, Ohio

Barbara Holliday • Kyle, Texas

Arlan Holthur • Auburn, Nebraska

Joan Hubbard • Marysville, California

Jessie Huntley • Clio, Michigan

Lucy Hyman • Albany, Georgia

Ethel Ince • Apache Junction, Arizona

Vera Ingram • Richmond, California

Janica Jackson • San Antonio, Texas

Mary and Ed Jakstis • North Grafton,
   Maryland

Maria Jeffers • San Antonio, Texas

Sylvia Jenkins • San Antonio, Texas

Nancy Jennings • Shawnee, Kansas

Lynda Jernigan • Universal City, Texas

Dorothy Jones • Mobile, Alabama

Frankie Jones • San Antonio, Texas

Ruth Jones • Fairborn, Ohio

Elizabeth Jordan • San Antonio, Texas

Esther Marie Judah • Mesa, Arizona

Ms. Marion King • San Antonio, Texas

Dee Dee Kloppe • San Antonio, Texas

Nancy Kohn • San Antonio, Texas

Amanda Katheryn Koontz • Hurst, Texas

Lois Kyker • Telford, Tennessee

Donis Laine • San Antonio, Texas

Diane McCall • Kingston Springs, Texas

Mildred McElfresh • San Antonio, Texas

Helen Staten McEvoy • Mesquite, Texas

Hazel McRae • Jordan, Montana

Elizabeth Magana • Lincoln Park,
   Michigan

Brenda Marcum • Indianapolis, Indiana

Ellie Marcum • Brooksville, Florida

Kay Marker • San Antonio, Texas

Dora Martin • St. Joseph, Missouri

Emmet Martin • San Antonio, Texas

Karen Martin • Gallup, New Mexico

Angie Matney • San Antonio, Texas

Ruth Maxwell • Forest City, North
   Carolina

Claire Mawyer • San Antonio, Texas

Lynn Miller • Ozark, Alabama

Marie Milheim • Houston, Texas

Bob Ann Moore • San Antonio, Texas

Ann Morisey • San Antonio, Texas

Velma Muniz • San Antonio, Texas

Pearl A. Nolf • Mineola, Texas

Lillian Nelson • St. Paul, Minnestoa

Sally Nelson • San Antonio, Texas

Pat Oelke • Fairmont, Minnesota

Joann Osborn • Monroe, Michigan

Jeannie Owens • Covington, Texas

Dee Pape • San Antonio, Texas

Joan Parker • San Antonio, Texas

David Pece

Hazel Pettit • Talala, Oklahoma

Judy Petty • Washington, Indiana

Rose M. Phillip • Phoenix, Arizona

Bertha Powers • Nederland, Texas

Ellen Preisler • Minneapolis, Minnesota

Ruth Pugh • Pensacola, Florida

Mary Putty • San Antonio, Texas

Elida Quinlisk • San Antonio, Texas

Jennifer Quintero • San Antonio, Texas

Robin Kay Rachall • Hurst, Texas

Faye Randall • San Antonio, Texas

Madeline Ray • Port St. Lucie, Florida

Eloise Reed • Brighton, Michigan

Jackie Renken • Austin, Texas

Luann Renken • Austin, Texas

Connie Ridings • San Antonio, Texas

Kathy Rigsby • San Antonio, Texas

Martha Holland Roberts • Tampa, Florida

Kay Robertson • San Antonio, Texas

Sue Robertson • San Antonio, Texas

Pat Romans • San Antonio, Texas

Wanda Rosson • San Antonio, Texas

Esther Sapp • San Diego, California

Helen Schaper • San Antonio, Texas

Dorothy Schumacher • Boerne, Texas

Annette Selcer • Kittering, Ohio

Jean Sharp • Cedar Creek, Texas

Johnnie Dolise Sheffield • Ace, Texas

Pauline Sheeks • Greenwood, Indiana

Marilyn Shipman • San Antonio, Texas

Mrs. Nard Shull • Ridgely, Tennessee

Elsie Skidmore • San Antonio, Texas

Joan Smith • Spindale, North Carolina

Hilda Smith • San Antonio, Texas

Winnie Smith • Northridge, California

Charlene Staffel • San Antonio, Texas

Jaycene Staffel • San Antonio, Texas

Lorene Stahl • San Antonio, Texas

Randie Stroh • Walsenburg, Colorado

Connie Stewart • Brea, California

Vi Stewart • San Antonio, Texas

Susan Marie Sundholm • Mineola, Texas

Louise Swanson • Stillman Valley, Illinois

Mrs. Harvey Taylor • Bradyville, Tennessee

Melissa Isom Taylor • San Antonio, Texas

Bonnie Thompson • San Antonio, Texas

Mary Ann Thompson • Boerne, Texas

Margie Tibbits • Greenwood, Louisiana

Linda Traywick • San Antonio, Texas

Laura Trombetta • New Port Richey, Florida

Barbara Trujillo • San Antonio, Texas

Anna Van Vliet • Dublin, Texas

Irma L. Violett • Neodesha, Kansas

Sheryl Visich • Vallejo, California

Jo Wagner • San Antonio, Texas

Lillian S. Wanslow • Bonham, Texas

John Ward • San Antonio, Texas

Claudine Wasson • Florissant, Missouri

Belle Wells • New Port Richey, Florida

Bessie Wentz • Hanover, Pennsylvania

Joan Werch • Camanche, Iowa

Peggy Werner • Bilington, West Virginia

Linda Wheeler • Georgetown, Illinois

Blanche Whetherhult • San Antonio, Texas

Juanita Wilcox • Shelbyville, Indiana

Janet Wilder • San Antonio, Texas

Vera Williams • Albuquerque, New Mexico

Brooke Escott Wilson • Palm Springs, California

Dorothy Whitaker • Somerset, Kentucky

Donna Woodie • Oklahoma City, Oklahoma

Lisa Worthington • Columbus, Ohio

Millie Wrightsman • San Antonio, Texas

Gloria Yirka • San Antonio, Texas

Sally Zaccaria • San Antonio, Texas

Index

Chicken

Chocolate

Ministry of Helps

N

O

P

Pasta

John Hagee Ministries
P. O. Box 1400
San Antonio, TX 78295-9951

Please send ____ copy(ies) of **Not By Bread Alone** @ $17.95 each_____

(B-31)   Total _____

Name_____

Address_____

City _____ State_____ Zip _____

Make checks payable to *John Hagee Ministries*

- -

John Hagee Ministries
P. O. Box 1400
San Antonio, TX 78295-9951

Please send ____ copy(ies) of **Not By Bread Alone** @ $17.95 each_____

(B-31)   Total _____

Name_____

Address_____

City _____ State_____ Zip _____

Make checks payable to *John Hagee Ministries*

- -

John Hagee Ministries
P. O. Box 1400
San Antonio, TX 78295-9951

Please send ____ copy(ies) of **Not By Bread Alone** @ $17.95 each_____

(B-31)   Total _____

Name_____

Address_____

City _____ State_____ Zip _____

Make checks payable to *John Hagee Ministries*